Sock-Yarn SHAWLS

15 Lacy Knitted Shawl Patterns

Jen Lucas

Martingale®
Create with Confidence

Dedication

To Alex, for believing in me.

Sock-Yarn Shawls: 15 Lacy Knitted Shawl Patterns
© 2013 by Jen Lucas

Martingale®
19021 120th Ave. NE, Ste. 102
Bothell, WA 98011-9511 USA
ShopMartingale.com

Printed in China
18 17 16 15 14   8 7 6 5

Library of Congress Cataloging-in-Publication Data is available upon request.

ISBN: 978-1-60468-194-9

Mission Statement

Dedicated to providing quality products and service to inspire creativity.

Credits

President & CEO: Tom Wierzbicki

Editor in Chief: Mary V. Green

Design Director: Paula Schlosser

Managing Editor: Karen Costello Soltys

Technical Editor: Ursula Reikes

Copy Editor: Marcy Heffernan

Production Manager: Regina Girard

Illustrator: Kathryn Conway

Cover & Text Designer: Regina Girard

Photographer: Brent Kane

Contents

Introduction

When I find something new that I love, I dive in head-first and quickly become obsessed. I do this with new music all the time. I hear a song by an artist on the radio while driving in my car, and the next thing I know I'm at home downloading every single song he or she has ever recorded. I do the same with knitting. First it was socks. I could not knit socks fast enough. I was constantly scouring the Internet for the newest, most-popular sock patterns. I would buy skein after skein of sock yarn, waiting for that perfect sock pattern to come along. Eventually my sock obsession somewhat subsided, and what was left was quite the stash of sock yarn. Not knowing what to do with all this yarn, I once again turned to the Internet. By this time, the community website Ravelry had entered the lives of knitters, making searching for things to do with your yarn one thousand times easier. It was then that I learned about people using sock yarn to knit small shawls.

A new knitting obsession grew. It continued to grow as I knit the same shawlette pattern four times before I had to finally stop myself. I was using up my sock-yarn stash fast, but now it was rarely for socks. My new love of small-shawl knitting grew so big that when an online class showing how to design your own shawl popped up on a well-known designer's website, it was an experience I didn't want to miss. Over the last couple of years since taking that class, my love of knitting small shawls with sock yarn hasn't abated, and it's led me to put together this book of patterns for the thing I love to knit the most.

The patterns in this book are organized in three sections—Lace-Edged Shawls, Allover-Lace Shawls, and Beyond-the-Triangle Shawls. In the first section, the shawls are all knit starting at the top center and worked outward. The shawls are worked in either garter or stockinette stitch, with a lace edging. This is a great place to start if you are new to knitting shawls and want to learn the basics of shawl construction.

The second section features patterns that have allover-lace motifs. The shawl may contain one allover-lace pattern with a complementing edge, or may feature several different motifs that flow together.

Finally, in Beyond-the-Triangle Shawls, you'll find shawls that are constructed a little bit differently. For example, one shawl is knit from the bottom up and uses short rows for shaping, while another is knit from side to side.

Most of the projects in this book can be completed with just one skein of sock yarn. The amount of yarn in a skein may vary from one brand or indie dyer to another, so be sure to check the pattern for yardage requirements. Some knitters love these small shawl patterns, while others may wish to make their shawls larger. In many of the patterns, look for a tip box on how to make the shawl larger if you have an extra skein of yarn.

I hope you enjoy knitting the patterns in this book. Maybe small-shawl knitting with sock yarn will become your new knitting obsession!

Choosing the Right Yarn

As a knitter, you have a love of yarn. Maybe you're the kind of knitter who doesn't have a yarn stash and just buys for each project as you need it. Or maybe you're more like me (and, I think, the majority of knitters), and you love to go to the yarn store and buy yarn to use "someday." For this second group of knitters, sock yarn can be very tempting. In this one subset of yarn, you can find just about anything you would ever want—from a strong, durable yarn that can be transformed into the perfect "work boot" socks to the softest, squishiest yarn that you would never dream of putting on someone's feet. Sock yarn can have sparkles, it can be stretchy, it can be solid, mottled, variegated, or hand dyed. The list goes on and on.

So how do you know what kind of sock yarn to pick for a shawl? Everyone's preferences are different, but there are a couple of things to think about that will make turning sock yarn into a shawl a success.

First, you always need to look at the yardage. Sock-yarn skeins can vary widely by company, and you want to make sure you go into your project with enough yarn. Some skeins of yarn might be only 150 to 200 yards, or you might find a skein that is 500 yards or more. So be sure to check those yarn labels! These days there are hundreds of amazing hand dyers selling yarn. Some dyers can reproduce colorways, and some cannot. Even for those that do reproduce colorways, there can be variances between dye lots. So, as for any project, you want to make sure you start with enough yarn in the same dye lot.

The second thing to consider for your shawl project is the color of the yarn. For allover-lace projects, I highly recommend using a solid or semisolid yarn. You can see the stitch pattern so much better with this type of yarn. If you pick a yarn that's highly variegated, you'll end up unable to see the lace motifs, especially large ones.

Sock yarns are available in a wide range of colors and fiber contents, making the choice for a shawl almost limitless.

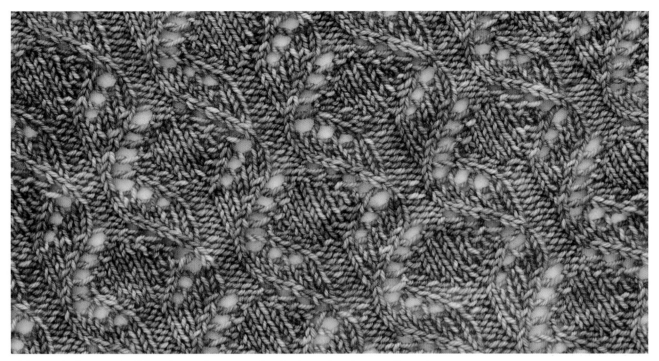

This mottled or semisolid teal yarn from Hazel Knits is perfect for an allover lace pattern.

If you're doing all that work to knit lace, you want people to be able to see it! I also prefer to use a yarn that's lighter in color, for no other reason than it's much easier to see what you're doing while knitting. There are times, though, when a variegated yarn will work just fine. For example, for the Harvey pattern (page 52), the shawl is composed of eyelets and garter stitch. That pattern can handle a multicolored yarn since the lace motif is small and simple.

Third, fiber content is a very important consideration for choosing the right yarn. Most sock yarns contain at least some wool. For shawls, I tend to look for a superwash merino, since the shawl will be worn around someone's neck, and non-superwash wool yarns can be a little itchier than other wool choices, especially in that sensitive area. Many companies have added merino/cashmere/nylon blends to their lines, and these are my favorites to use for knitting shawls. They're so soft, and the finished shawls block like a dream. But what if the shawl recipient is allergic to wool or other animal fibers? Fortunately, there are lots of sock yarns that don't contain any animal fibers at all. If you're going for a yarn that's totally free of animal fiber, look for one that isn't 100% cotton. Cotton can be hard to block and doesn't hold its shape well over time. Many cotton blends, however, work great for shawl knitting. Other blends containing bamboo, Tencel, nylon, and even milk protein fiber (yes, milk!) can also be great choices.

Ultimately, the yarn you choose is entirely up to you; however, using some of the suggestions here will help make your shawl-knitting experience a success.

A NOTE ABOUT GAUGE

All gauges listed in this book are based on a washed, blocked swatch. Take time to check your gauge so you don't run out of yarn!

Reading Charts

Chart reading can be very overwhelming to a knitter—especially in lace projects. The charts can be odd shaped, there are many different symbols within them, and sometimes you'll need to follow several charts during the course of knitting a shawl. While this book includes written instructions as well as charts for each project, here are a few quick tips if you're attempting chart reading for the first time.

Charts start at the bottom right-hand corner. Notice the number 1 in the bottom right-hand corner of the following chart.

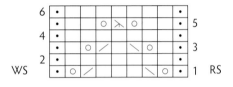

This indicates that this is the first row and tells you where to start knitting. You read the chart from right to left, just as you knit the stitches off your needle from right to left. Once row 1 is complete, you'll work back across on the wrong side of the work. You'll notice that the 2, which indicates row 2 in the above chart, is on the left side. The row number on the left side of the chart is your indication that you're knitting on the wrong side. Read the chart from left to right on that row.

Now that you know where to start and how to proceed, you need to know what the symbols all mean. There is some standardization, but every designer may have a slight variation of the symbols. Be sure to check the key, which will explain what each symbol stands for. Stitch names are abbreviated, but you can see what the abbreviations mean on page 76.

Key

• P on RS, K on WS	☐ K on RS, P on WS
○ YO	╱ K2tog
╲ Ssk	⋉ SK2P

The key tells you exactly what to do as you come to each symbol. Going back to row 1 of the chart on the left, you can see that it will be worked as P1, YO, ssk, K3, K2tog, YO, P1. Row 2 will be worked as K1, P7, K1.

When knitting a shawl, the chart will often grow much like the shawl will grow as you increase stitches and work toward the bottom edge. A typical chart and key for a shawl pattern may look like this.

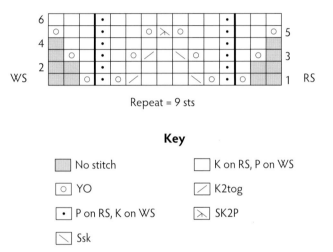

Repeat = 9 sts

Key

▨ No stitch	☐ K on RS, P on WS
○ YO	╱ K2tog
• P on RS, K on WS	⋉ SK2P
╲ Ssk	

This chart will be worked back and forth in the same way, but there are a couple of additional considerations when working charts to knit a shawl.

The first thing to look at is the "no stitch" symbol. This can be indicated by a grayed-out box, or sometimes by an empty space before the first stitch is worked. Don't despair that you may be missing stitches. On the subsequent rows you'll be increasing and adding stitches where there weren't stitches in previous rows. In the above example, the increasing occurs by adding yarn overs at the beginning and end of the rows.

Second, it is very common in shawl knitting that a set of stitches will need to be repeated several times across a row. Again, looking at the above example, you'll notice a set of stitches between the bold vertical lines. Underneath the chart, it indicates that these stitches are repeated, as well as the number of stitches within that repeat. Take a look at chart row 3 above. Written out, it's: YO, K1 *P1, K1, YO, ssk, K1, K2tog, YO, K1, P1; rep from * to last st, K1, YO. The section of the chart that is between the two bold vertical lines is the section of the written pattern between the * and the semicolon.

Finally, with shawl knitting, the charts may show only the patterned sections of the shawl to knit, so you need to carefully read the entire pattern to get the whole story. In many of the patterns in this book, you'll see instructions written as follows:

Cont working first 3 sts and last 3 sts in garter st (knit every row). Cont working the center st in St st (knit on RS, purl on WS). In between st markers, work chart A on each half of shawl.

This means that the edge stitches and center stitch are not accounted for on the chart. For some of the larger lace projects, if a chart showed the whole row for the shawl, the chart would be so big that it would have to be shrunk to an unreadable size just to fit on a page in this book! To avoid this, the simple edge and center stitches are not included in the chart; only the lace portions are charted, making the chart more manageable.

So, don't let those charts scare you. If you're looking to use a chart for the first time, I recommend starting with one of the lace-edged shawls, which contains only one or two charts used for the edge of the shawl. Or try the Harvey pattern (page 52). Only one small chart is used for that shawl, and it's repeated several times. With a little practice, you can soon be knitting shawls almost entirely from the charts.

Using Stitch Markers

If you're new to lace knitting, stitch markers can be a very useful tool. They can help keep your place in your knitting and provide a quick visual guide when you come back to your knitting after time away.

Choosing Stitch Markers

Many types of stitch markers are available, and knitters have a wide variety of preferences when it comes to choosing which ones to use. Some of the least-expensive and most-readily available stitch markers are plastic locking stitch markers. These are great for when you need to move the markers around between each lace repeat, as explained on page 10.

Another inexpensive option is the split-ring marker. While these stitch markers have lots of great uses, they're not the best choice when it comes to lace knitting. Because of the split in the markers, every now and then they can catch on the yarn, potentially leaving you confused and unsure of your place. That is never good when knitting lace!

Some markers are promoted as snag free. Found on the handmade-product website Etsy and other websites, these are my favorite markers for working on basic shawl projects. Their smooth edges won't catch on

your yarn, and they slip easily and quickly on and off the needles.

Decorative stitch markers aren't a necessity, but they can make your knitting experience more fun. On Etsy, you can find tons of markers that will dangle from your needles beautifully.

If you haven't used stitch markers before, try a few different types to figure out your preference.

Stitch markers, clockwise from top left: locking, split-ring, snag-free, and decorative.

Moving Stitch Markers

So you've selected your stitch markers; now the question is, where to place them? Many of the patterns in this book use stitch markers to mark the edge stitches and center stitches. Marking these stitches (especially the center ones) is helpful so that you know when to stop repeating a chart and when to switch charts.

When it comes to repeating a set of stitches across a row, some knitters find it helpful to place a stitch marker after each repeat. You can end up with a lot of stitch markers on the needle when you do this, but it can help you keep track of where you are in the pattern. However, placing a stitch marker after each repeat in the row can sometimes cause issues. Depending on how the lace pattern is set up, you may have to "borrow a stitch" from the next repeat in order to complete the repeat you're working. This can be a little confusing, so let's look at an example.

When working the following chart, you'll have to borrow a stitch from the next repeat when each repeat is separated by a stitch marker.

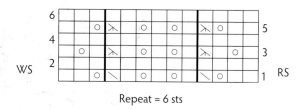

Repeat = 6 sts

When working the first row of the pattern, place the stitch markers at each repeat. You work the second row on the wrong side by simply slipping the markers along the way. When you reach the third row, it will be time to borrow a stitch. At the first double decrease you'll only have two stitches left before the marker, but you need three stitches in order to complete that stitch.

Three stitches are needed to complete the double increase, but only two stitches are before the marker.

Remove the stitch marker, complete the double-decrease stitch, and then place the stitch marker on the right needle.

Here the marker was removed, the stitch completed, and the marker placed back on the needle.

Repeat this process across the row, moving the stitch marker at each repeat. This is where those locking stitch markers come in handy—you just unclasp them, complete the stitch, and slip them back onto the needle. With other stitch markers, you'll have to slip stitches back and forth in order to remove the markers, which takes some extra time and can lead to the dreaded dropped stitch.

Whether you decide to use lots of stitch markers or none at all is entirely up to you. If you do choose to add stitch markers at each repeat, hopefully this explanation of how to move them around when necessary will lead you to successful shawl knitting.

Lace-Edged Shawls

The five shawls in this section all start from the top center and are worked outward. They feature either a stockinette- or garter-stitch body, with a pretty little lace detail worked on the edge. If you've never knit a shawl before, this is a great place to start. You'll understand the basic concept of triangular shawl construction and have a lovely little lace shawl as the result.

Inflorescence

This shawl flows from
stockinette into a lacy floral
pattern. Love the look of the
lace at the edge of the shawl?
With a second skein of yarn
you can make the lace section
bigger and turn a flower bed
into a whole garden!

SKILL LEVEL: Intermediate ⬤⬛⬛▢

FINISHED MEASUREMENTS: 60" x 26"

Materials

1 skein of Heritage from Cascade Yarns (75% superwash merino wool, 25% nylon; 100 g; 437 yds) in color 5640 Rust ⓵

US size 4 (3.5 mm) circular needle, 24" or longer

4 stitch markers

Tapestry needle

Blocking wires and/or blocking pins

Gauge

20 sts and 32 rows = 4" in St st

Lace Patterns

See charts A, B, and C on page 15, or follow written instructions below.

Chart A

Row 1 (RS): YO, K1, YO, ssk, K3, *K4, K2tog, YO, K1, YO, ssk, K3; rep from * to 7 sts before marker, K4, K2tog, YO, K1, YO.

Row 2 and all even-numbered rows (WS): Purl all sts.

Row 3: YO, K3, YO, ssk, K2, *K3, K2tog, YO, K3, YO, ssk, K2; rep from * to 8 sts before marker, K3, K2tog, YO, K3, YO.

Row 5: YO, K2tog, YO, K1, (YO, ssk) twice, K1, *K2, (K2tog, YO) twice, K1, (YO, ssk) twice, K1; rep from * to 9 sts before marker, K2, (K2tog, YO) twice, K1, YO, ssk, YO.

Row 7: YO, K2tog, YO, K3, (YO, ssk) twice, *K1, (K2tog, YO) twice, K3, (YO, ssk) twice; rep from * to 10 sts before marker, K1, (K2tog, YO) twice, K3, YO, ssk, YO.

Row 8: Purl all sts.

Chart B

Row 1 (RS): YO, K4, YO, K1, YO, K3, K2tog, *K1, ssk, K3, YO, K1, YO, K3, K2tog; rep from * to 11 sts before marker, K1, ssk, K3, YO, K1, YO, K4, YO.

Row 2 and all even-numbered rows (WS): Purl all sts.

Row 3: YO, K5, YO, K3, YO, K2, K2tog, *K1, ssk, K2, YO, K3, YO, K2, K2tog; rep from * to 13 sts before marker, K1, ssk, K2, YO, K3, YO, K5, YO.

Row 5: YO, K2, *(K1, YO, ssk) twice, (K1, K2tog, YO) twice; rep from * to 3 sts before marker, K3, YO.

Row 7: YO, K3, *K2, YO, ssk, K1, YO, SK2P, YO, K1, K2tog, YO, K1; rep from * to 4 sts before marker, K4, YO.

Row 9: YO, K2, K2tog, YO, *K1, (YO, ssk) twice, K3, (K2tog, YO) twice; rep from * to 5 sts before marker, K1, YO, ssk, K2, YO.

Row 11: YO, K2, K2tog, YO, K1, *K2, (YO, ssk) twice, K1, (K2tog, YO) twice, K1; rep from * to 6 sts before marker, K2, YO, ssk, K2, YO.

Row 12: Purl all sts.

Chart C

Row 1 (RS): YO, K1, ssk, K3, YO, *K1, YO, K3, K2tog, K1, ssk, K3, YO; rep from * to 7 sts before marker, K1, YO, K3, K2tog, K1, YO.

Row 2 and all even-numbered rows (WS): Purl all sts.

Row 3: YO, K2, ssk, K2, YO, K1, *K2, YO, K2, K2tog, K1, ssk, K2, YO, K1; rep from * to 8 sts before marker, K2, YO, K2, K2tog, K2, YO.

Row 5: YO, K3, YO, ssk, K1, YO, ssk, *(K1, K2tog, YO) twice, (K1, YO, ssk) twice; rep from * to 9 sts before marker, (K1, K2tog, YO) twice, K3, YO.

Row 7: YO, K5, YO, ssk, K1, YO, *SK2P, YO, K1, K2tog, YO, K3, YO, ssk, K1, YO; rep from * to 11 sts before marker, SK2P, YO, K1, K2tog, YO, K5, YO.

Row 9: YO, (K2tog, YO) twice, K1, (YO, ssk) twice, K1, *K2, (K2tog, YO) twice, K1, (YO, ssk) twice, K1; rep from * to 11 sts before marker, K2, (K2tog, YO) twice, K1, (YO, ssk) twice, YO.

Row 11: YO, (K2tog, YO) twice, K3, (YO, ssk) twice, *K1, (K2tog, YO) twice, K3, (YO, ssk) twice; rep from * to 12 sts before marker, K1, (K2tog, YO) twice, K3, (YO, ssk) twice, YO.

Row 13: YO, *K1, ssk, K3, YO, K1, YO, K3, K2tog; rep from * to last st before marker, K1, YO.

Row 15: YO, K1, *K1, ssk, K2, YO, K3, YO, K2, K2tog; rep from * to 2 sts before marker, K2, YO.

Row 17: YO, K2tog, YO, *(K1, YO, ssk) twice, (K1, K2tog, YO) twice; rep from * to 3 sts before marker, K1, YO, ssk, YO.

Row 19: YO, K2tog, YO, K1, *K2, YO, ssk, K1, YO, SK2P, YO, K1, K2tog, YO, K1; rep from * to 4 sts before marker, K2, YO, ssk, YO.

Row 21: YO, (K2tog, YO) twice, *K1, (YO, ssk) twice, K3, (K2tog, YO) twice; rep from * to 5 sts before marker, K1, (YO, ssk) twice, YO.

Row 23: YO, (K2tog, YO) twice, K1, *K2, (YO, ssk) twice, K1, (K2tog, YO) twice, K1; rep from * to 6 sts before marker, K2, (YO, ssk) twice, YO.

Body of Shawl

Work tab CO (page 74) as foll: CO 3 sts. Knit 6 rows. Turn work 90° and pick up 3 sts along edge. Turn work 90° and pick up 3 sts from CO edge. (9 sts)

Row 1 (RS): K3, PM, YO, K1, YO, PM, K1 (center st), PM, YO, K1, YO, PM, K3. (13 sts)

Row 2 (WS): K3, purl to last 3 sts (slipping markers), K3.

Row 3: K3, SM, YO, knit to next marker, YO, SM, K1, SM, YO, knit to last 3 sts, YO, SM, K3.

Work rows 2 and 3 another 52 times. Rep row 2 once more. (225 sts)

Lace Edging

Cont working first 3 sts and last 3 sts in garter st (knit every row), and center st in St st (knit on RS, purl on WS). Work chart A between st markers on each half of shawl. (241 sts)

Work chart B between st markers on each half of shawl. (273 sts)

Work chart C between st markers on each half of shawl. (321 sts)

> **MAKE IT BIGGER!**
>
> *If you have a second skein of yarn, repeat chart A and chart B one more time before moving on to chart C to add some length to your shawl.*

Finishing

BO loosely purlwise as described on page 75. With tapestry needle, weave in ends. Using blocking wires or pins, block to finished measurements.

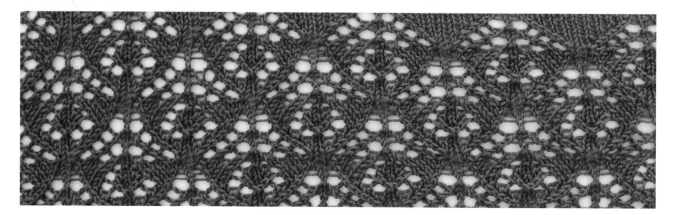

Chart A

Repeat = 12 sts

Beg sts

End sts

Rows (right side): 7, 5, 3, 1
Rows (left side): 8, 6, 4, 2

Chart B

Repeat = 12 sts

Beg sts

End sts

Rows (right side): 11, 9, 7, 5, 3, 1
Rows (left side): 12, 10, 8, 6, 4, 2

Chart C

Repeat = 12 sts

Beg sts

End sts

Rows (right side): 23, 21, 19, 17, 15, 13, 11, 9, 7, 5, 3, 1
Rows (left side): 22, 20, 18, 16, 14, 12, 10, 8, 6, 4, 2

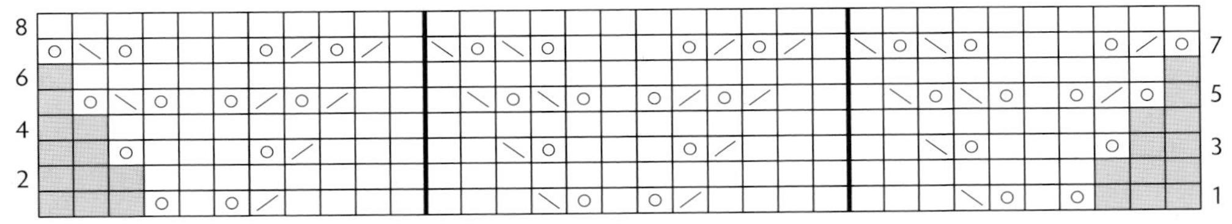

Key

⊙	YO
□	K on RS, P on WS
╱	Ssk
╲	K2tog
⅄	SK2P
▨	No stitch

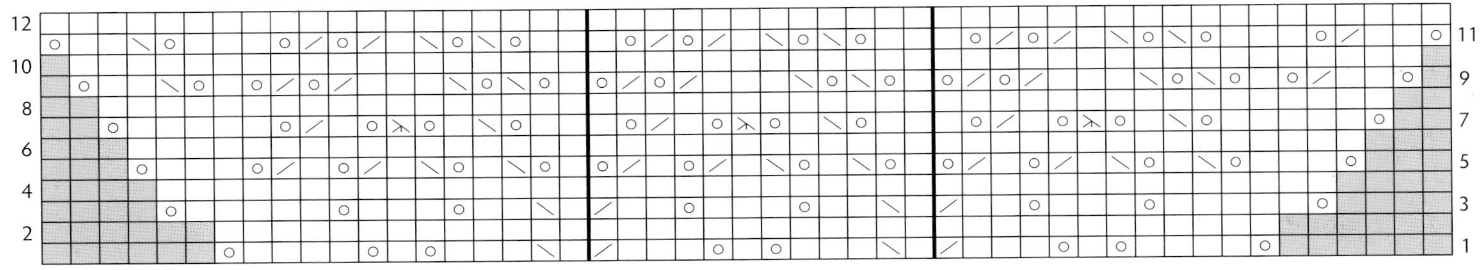

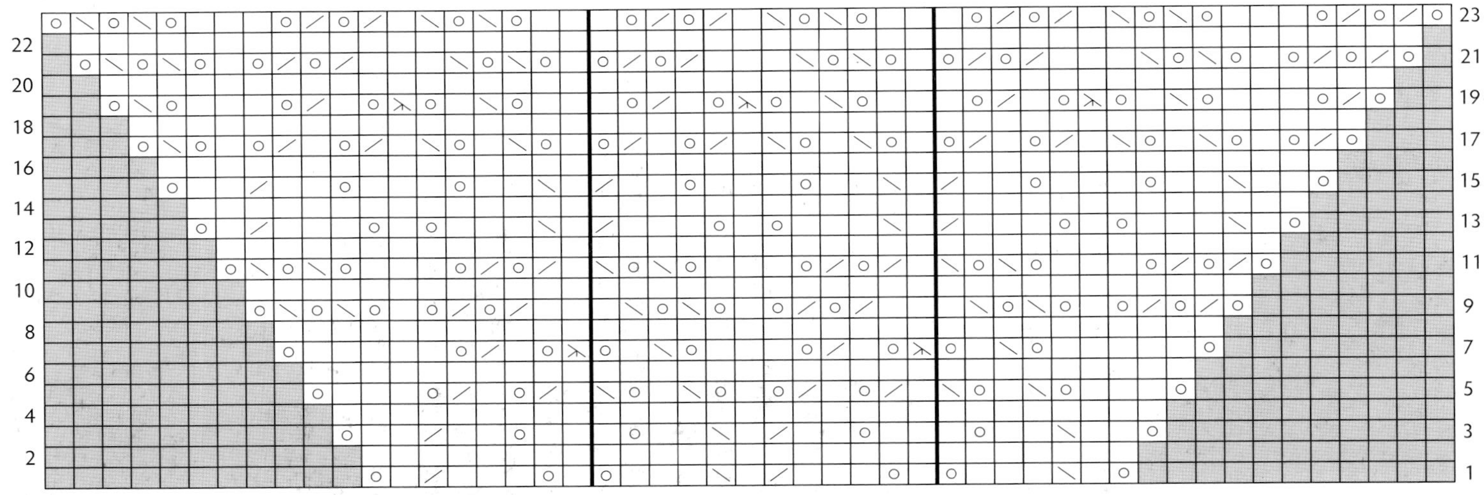

Ladybug

Use your imagination and look closely at the lace. Could there be ladybugs climbing along the edge of this pretty, airy shawlette?

SKILL LEVEL: Intermediate ■■■□

FINISHED MEASUREMENTS: 50" x 21"

Materials

1 skein of Foot Notes from Fiber Optic Yarns (80% superwash merino wool, 20% nylon; 114 g; 420 yds) in color Batik (●1)

US size 4 (3.5 mm) circular needle, 24" or longer

4 stitch markers

Tapestry needle

Blocking wires and/or blocking pins

Gauge

20 sts and 34 rows = 4" in St st

Lace Patterns

See charts A and B on page 18, or follow written instructions below.

Chart A

Row 1 (RS): YO, K1, *ssk, K3, YO, K1, YO, K3, K2tog, K1; rep from * to marker, YO.

Row 2 and all even-numbered rows (WS): Purl all sts.

Row 3: YO, K2, *ssk, K2, YO, K3, YO, K2, K2tog, K1; rep from * to 1 st before marker, K1, YO.

Row 5: YO, K3, *ssk, K1, YO, K5, YO, K1, K2tog, K1; rep from * to 2 sts before marker, K2, YO.

Row 7: YO, K3, YO, K1, *YO, K3, K2tog, P1, ssk, K3, YO, K1; rep from * to 3 sts before marker, YO, K3, YO.

Row 9: (YO, K2) 3 times, *K1, YO, K2, K2tog, P1, ssk, K2, YO, K2; rep from * to 5 sts before marker, K1, YO, (K2, YO) twice.

Row 11: (YO, K2) 3 times, YO, K3, *K2, YO, K1, K2tog, P1, ssk, K1, YO, K3; rep from * to 8 sts before marker, (K2, YO) 4 times.

Row 12: Purl all sts.

Rep rows 1–12 for patt.

Chart B

Row 1 (RS): YO, K1, *K1, YO, K1, K2tog, P3, ssk, K1, YO, K2; rep from * to marker, YO.

Row 2 and all even-numbered rows (WS): Purl all sts.

Row 3: (YO, K1) twice, *K1, YO, K2tog, P5, ssk, YO, K2; rep from * to 1 st before marker, YO, K1, YO.

Row 5: (YO, K2) twice, *K1, YO, K1, ssk, P3, K2tog, K1, YO, K2; rep from * to 3 sts before marker, K1, YO, K2, YO.

Row 7: YO, K1, YO, K2tog, YO, K1, YO, SK2P, *(YO, K1) twice, ssk, P1, K2tog, (K1, YO) twice, SK2P; rep from * to 4 sts before marker, YO, K1, YO, ssk, YO, K1, YO.

Row 9: YO, K2, YO, K2tog, (YO, K1) twice, SK2P, *(K1, YO) twice, K1, SK2P; rep from * to 6 sts before marker, (K1, YO) twice, ssk, YO, K2, YO.

Body of Shawl

Work tab CO (page 74) as foll: CO 3 sts. Knit 6 rows. Turn work 90° and pick up 3 sts along edge. Turn work 90° and pick up 3 sts from CO edge. (9 sts total)

Row 1 (RS): K3, PM, YO, K1, YO, PM, K1 (center st), PM, YO, K1, YO, PM, K3. (13 sts)

Row 2 (WS): K3, purl to last 3 sts (slipping markers), K3.

Row 3: K3, SM, YO, knit to next marker, YO, SM, K1, SM, YO, knit to last 3 sts, YO, SM, K3.

Work rows 2 and 3 another 34 times. Rep row 2 once more. (153 sts)

Lace Edging

Cont working first 3 sts and last 3 sts in garter st (knit every row). Cont working center st in St st (knit on RS, purl on WS). Work chart A between st markers on each half of shawl 3 times total.

Stitch Count	
First rep of chart A	201 sts
Second rep of chart A	249 sts
Third rep of chart A	297 sts

MAKE IT BIGGER!

With extra yarn, you can continue working chart A as many times as you like before moving on to chart B.

Work chart B in between st markers on each half of shawl. (333 sts)

Finishing

BO loosely purlwise, using method described on page 75. With tapestry needle, weave in ends. Using blocking wires or pins, block to finished measurements.

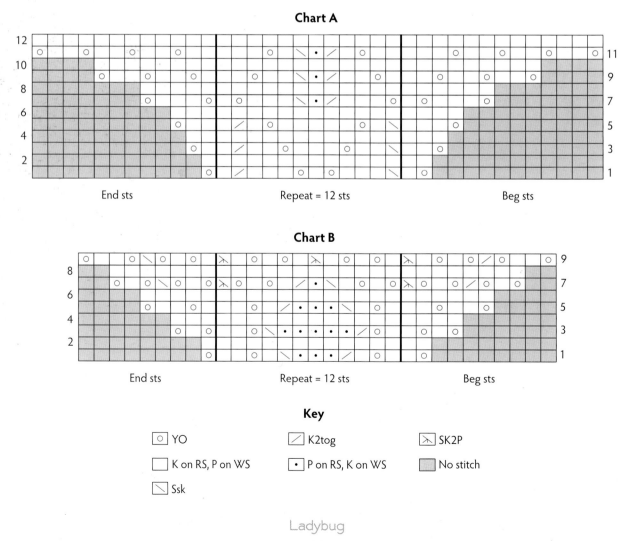

Chart A

End sts   Repeat = 12 sts   Beg sts

Chart B

End sts   Repeat = 12 sts   Beg sts

Key

◯ YO   ╱ K2tog   ⋌ SK2P

☐ K on RS, P on WS   • P on RS, K on WS   ▨ No stitch

╲ Ssk

Ardor

Garter-stitch shawls are a great introduction to shawl knitting. Watch the easy garter-stitch portion grow on your needles, and then add a simple lace detail at the end. Try knitting one with a semisolid sock yarn for a rich, cozy shawl.

SKILL LEVEL: Intermediate ■■■□

FINISHED MEASUREMENTS: 54" x 25"

Materials

1 skein of Solemate from Lorna's Laces (55% superwash merino wool, 15% nylon, 30% Outlast viscose; 100 g; 425 yds) in color Kerfuffle (**1**)

US size 5 (3.75 mm) circular needle, 24" or longer

Tapestry needle

Blocking wires and/or blocking pins

Gauge

20 sts and 32 rows = 4" in garter st

Lace Patterns

See charts A and B on page 22, or follow written instructions below.

Chart A

Rows 1 and 3 (RS): K3, YO, knit to center st, YO, K1, YO, knit to last 3 sts, YO, K3.

Rows 2 and 4 (WS): Knit all sts.

Row 5: K3, YO, K2, *ssk, K4, YO, K1, YO, K2tog; rep from * to 2 sts before center st, K2, YO, K1 (center st, YO, K2, **ssk, YO, K1, YO, K4, K2tog; rep from ** to last 5 sts, K2, YO, K3.

Rows 6, 8, 10, and 12: K3, purl to last 3 sts, K3.

Row 7: K3, YO, K3, *ssk, K3, (YO, K1) twice, K2tog; rep from * to 3 sts from center st, K3, YO, K1, YO, K3, **ssk, (K1, YO) twice, K3, K2tog; rep from ** to last 6 sts, K3, YO, K3.

Row 9: K3, YO, K4, *ssk, K2, YO, K1, YO, K2, K2tog; rep from * to 4 sts before center st, K4, YO, K1, YO, K4, **ssk, K2, YO, K1, YO, K2, K2tog; rep from ** to last 7 sts, K4, YO, K3.

Row 11: K3, YO, K2, YO, ssk, YO, K1, *ssk, (K1, YO) twice, K3, K2tog; rep from * to 5 sts before center st, K1, YO, K2tog, YO, K2, YO, K1, YO, K2, YO, ssk, YO, K1, **ssk, K3, (YO, K1) twice, K2tog; rep from ** to last 8 sts, K1, YO, K2tog, YO, K2, YO, K3.

Row 13: (K3, YO) twice, ssk, YO, K2, *ssk, YO, K1, YO, K4, K2tog; rep from * to 7 sts before center st, K2, YO, K2tog, YO, K3, YO, K1, YO, K3, YO, ssk, YO, K2, **ssk, K4, YO, K1, YO, K2tog; rep from ** to last 10 sts, K2, YO, K2tog, (YO, K3) twice.

Row 14: K3, purl to last 3 sts, K3.

Rep rows 1–14 for patt.

Chart B

Rows 1 and 3 (RS): K3, YO, knit to center st, YO, K1, YO, knit to last 3 sts, YO, K3.

Rows 2 and 4 (WS): Knit all sts.

Row 5: K3, YO, K2, *ssk, YO, K1, YO, SK2P, YO, K1, YO, K2tog; rep from * to 2 sts before the center st, K2, YO, K1, YO, K2, **ssk, YO, K1, YO, SK2P, YO, K1, YO, K2tog; rep from ** to last 5 sts, K2, YO, K3.

Rows 6, 8, 10, and 12: K3, purl to last 3 sts, K3.

Row 7: K3, YO, K1, YO, K2tog, *ssk, YO, K1, YO, SK2P, YO, K1, YO, K2tog; rep from * to 3 sts before center st, ssk, (YO, K1) 3 times, YO, K2tog, **ssk, YO, K1, YO, SK2P, YO, K1, YO, K2tog; rep from ** to last 6 sts, ssk, YO, K1, YO, K3.

Row 9: K3, YO, K2, YO, K2tog, *ssk, YO, K1, YO, SK2P, YO, K1, YO, K2tog; rep from * to 4 sts before center st, ssk, YO, K2, YO, K1, YO, K2, YO, K2tog, **ssk, YO, K1, YO, SK2P, YO, K1, YO, K2tog; rep from ** to last 7 sts, ssk, YO, K2, YO, K3.

Row 11: (K3, YO) twice, K2tog, *ssk, YO, K1, YO, SK2P, YO, K1, YO, K2tog; rep from * to 5 sts before center st, ssk, YO, K3, YO, K1, YO, K3, YO, K2tog, **ssk, YO, K1, YO, SK2P, YO, K1, YO, K2tog; rep from ** to last 8 sts, ssk, (YO, K3) twice.

Row 13: K3, YO, K4, YO, K2tog, *ssk, YO, K1, YO, SK2P, YO, K1, YO, K2tog; rep from * to 6 sts before center st, ssk, YO, K4, YO, K1, YO, K4, YO, K2tog, **ssk, YO, K1, YO, SK2P, YO, K1, YO, K2tog; rep from ** to last 9 sts, ssk, YO, K4, YO, K3.

Body of Shawl

Work tab CO (page 74) as foll: CO 3 sts. Knit 6 rows. Turn work 90° and pick up 3 sts along edge. Turn work 90° and pick up 3 sts from CO edge. (9 sts)

Row 1 (RS): K3, YO, K1, YO, K1 (center st), YO, K1, YO, K3. (13 sts)

Row 2 (WS): Knit all sts.

Row 3: K3, YO, knit to center st, YO, K1, YO, knit to last 3 sts, YO, K3.

Work rows 2 and 3 another 38 times. Rep row 2 once more. (169 sts)

Lace Edging

Work chart A twice. (205 sts after first rep; 241 sts after second)

Work chart B once. (269 sts)

MAKE IT BIGGER!

With extra yarn, you can repeat the 14 rows of chart A as many times as you like before moving on to chart B.

Finishing

BO loosely purlwise, using method described on page 75. With tapestry needle, weave in ends. Using blocking wires or pins, block to finished measurements.

Chart A

End sts · Middle sts · Repeat = 9 sts · Beg sts

Rows: 14, 12, 10, 8, 6, 4, 2 (left side) · 1, 3, 5, 7, 9, 11, 13 (right side)

Chart B

End sts · Middle sts · Repeat = 9 sts · Beg sts

Rows: 12, 10, 8, 6, 4, 2 (left side) · 1, 3, 5, 7, 9, 11, 13 (right side)

Key:

☐	K on RS, P on WS
•	P on RS, K on WS
○	YO
╱	Ssk
⋋	SK2P
╲	K2tog
▨	No stitch

Timpani

The rhythmic chevron lace pattern is sure to make this an addictive project. The stockinette body of the shawl flows into a geometric pattern that will leave you mesmerized.

SKILL LEVEL: Intermediate ■■■□

FINISHED MEASUREMENTS: 51" x 21"

Materials

2 skeins of Gloss from Knit Picks (70% merino wool, 30% silk; 50 g; 220 yds) in color Kenai ❶

US size 5 (3.75 mm) circular needle, 24" or longer

Tapestry needle

Blocking wires and/or blocking pins

Gauge

20 sts and 32 rows = 4" in St st

Lace Patterns

See charts A, B, and C on page 26, or follow written instructions below.

Chart A

Row 1 (RS): K3, YO, *K2, YO, ssk, K3, K2tog, YO, K3; rep from * to 1 st before center st, (K1, YO) twice, K1, **K3, YO, ssk, K3, K2tog, YO, K2; rep from ** to last 3 sts, YO, K3.

Row 2 and all even-numbered rows (WS): K3, purl to last 3 sts, K3.

Row 3: K3, YO, K1, *K3, YO, ssk, K1, K2tog, YO, K1, YO, ssk, K1; rep from * to 2 sts before center st, K2, YO, K1, YO, K2, **K1, K2tog, YO, K1, YO, ssk, K1, K2tog, YO, K3; rep from ** to last 4 sts, K1, YO, K3.

Row 5: K3, YO, K2, *K4, YO, SK2P, YO, K3, YO, ssk; rep from * to 3 sts before center st, K3, YO, K1, YO, K3, **K2tog, YO, K3, YO, SK2P, YO, K4; rep from ** to last 5 sts, K2, YO, K3.

Row 7: K3, YO, K2, YO, *ssk, K3, K2tog, YO, K5, YO; rep from * to 5 sts before center st, ssk, K3, YO, K1, YO, K3, K2tog, **YO, K5, YO, ssk, K3, K2tog; rep from ** to last 5 sts, YO, K2, YO, K3.

Row 9: K3, YO, K1, K2tog, YO, K1, *YO, ssk, K1, K2tog, YO, K4, K2tog, YO, K1; rep from * to 5 sts before center st, YO, ssk, K3, YO, K1, YO, K3, K2tog, YO, **K1, YO, ssk, K4, YO, ssk, K1, K2tog, YO; rep from ** to last 7 sts, K1, YO, ssk, K1, YO, K3.

Row 11: K3, YO, K1, K2tog, YO, K2, *K1, YO, SK2P, YO, K4, K2tog, YO, K2; rep from * to 6 sts before center st, K1, YO, SK2P, YO, K2, YO, K1, YO, K2, YO, SK2P, YO, K1, **K2, YO, ssk, K4, YO, SK2P, YO, K1; rep from ** to last 8 sts, K2, YO, ssk, K1, YO, K3.

Row 12: K3, purl to last 3 sts, K3.

Chart B

Row 1 (RS): K3, YO, K1, K2tog, YO, K3, *K2, YO, ssk, K3, K2tog, YO, K3; rep from * to 7 sts before center st, K2, YO, ssk, K3, YO, K1, YO, K3, K2tog, YO, K2, **K3, YO, ssk, K3, K2tog, YO, K2; rep from ** to last 9 sts, K3, YO, ssk, K1, YO, K3.

Row 2 and all even-numbered rows (WS): K3, purl to last 3 sts, K3.

Row 3: K3, YO, K1, K2tog, YO, K1, YO, ssk, K1, *K3, YO, ssk, K1, K2tog, YO, K1, YO, ssk, K1; rep from * to 8 sts before center st, K3, YO, ssk, K3, YO, K1, YO, K3, K2tog, YO, K3, **K1, K2tog, YO, K1, YO, ssk, K1, K2tog, YO, K3; rep from ** to last 10 sts, K1, K2tog, YO, K1, YO, ssk, K1, YO, K3.

Row 5: K3, YO, K1, K2tog, YO, K3, YO, ssk, *K4, YO, SK2P, YO, K3, YO, ssk; rep from * to 9 sts before center st, K4, YO, SK2P, YO, K2, YO, K1, YO, K2, YO, SK2P, YO, K4, **K2tog, YO, K3, YO, SK2P, YO, K4; rep from ** to last 11 sts, K2tog, YO, K3, YO, ssk, K1, YO, K3.

Row 7: K3, YO, K1, K2tog, YO, K5, YO, *ssk, K3, K2tog, YO, K5, YO; rep from * to 11 sts before center st, ssk, K3, K2tog, YO, K4, YO, K1, YO, K4, YO, ssk, K3, K2tog, **YO, K5, YO, ssk, K3, K2tog; rep from ** to last 11 sts, YO, K5, YO, ssk, K1, YO, K3.

Row 9: K3, YO, K1, K2tog, YO, K4, K2tog, YO, K1, *YO, ssk, K1, K2tog, YO, K4, K2tog, YO, K1; rep from * to 11 sts before center st, YO, ssk, K1, K2tog, YO, K6, YO, K1, YO, K6, YO, ssk, K1, K2tog, YO, **K1, YO, ssk, K4, YO, ssk, K1, K2tog, YO; rep from ** to last 13 sts, K1, YO, ssk, K4, YO, ssk, K1, YO, K3.

Row 11: K3, YO, K1, K2tog, YO, K4, K2tog, YO, K2, *K1, YO, SK2P, YO, K4, K2tog, YO, K2; rep from * to 12 sts before center st, K1, YO, SK2P, YO, K4, K2tog, YO, K2, YO, K1, YO, K2, YO, ssk, K4, YO, SK2P, YO, K1, **K2, YO, ssk, K4, YO, SK2P, YO, K1; rep from ** to last 14 sts, K2, YO, ssk, K4, YO, ssk, K1, YO, K3.

Row 12: K3, purl to last 3 sts, K3.

Chart C

Row 1 (RS): K3, YO, K1, K2tog, YO, K3, *K2, YO, ssk, K3, K2tog, YO, K3; rep from * to 7 sts before center st, K2, YO, ssk, K3, YO, K1, YO, K3, K2tog, YO, K2, **K3, YO, ssk, K3, K2tog, YO, K2; rep from ** to last 9 sts, K3, YO, ssk, K1, YO, K3.

Row 2 and all even-numbered rows (WS): K3, purl to last 3 sts, K3.

Row 3: K3, YO, K1, K2tog, YO, K1, YO, ssk, K1, *K3, YO, ssk, K1, K2tog, YO, K1, YO, ssk, K1; rep from * to 8 sts before center st, K3, YO, ssk, K3, YO, K1, YO, K3, K2tog, YO, K3, **K1, K2tog, YO, K1, YO, ssk, K1, K2tog, YO, K3; rep from ** to last 10 sts, K1, K2tog, YO, K1, YO, ssk, K1, YO, K3.

Row 5: K3, YO, K1, (K2tog, YO) twice, K1, YO, ssk, *K4, YO, SK2P, YO, K2tog, YO, K1, YO, ssk; rep from * to 9 sts before center st, K4, YO, SK2P, YO, K2, YO, K1, YO, K2, YO, SK2P, YO, K4, **K2tog, YO, K1, YO, ssk, YO, SK2P, YO, K4; rep from ** to last 11 sts, K2tog, YO, K1, (YO, ssk) twice, K1, YO, K3.

Row 7: K3, YO, K1, (K2tog, YO) 3 times, K1, YO, *ssk, K3, (K2tog, YO) 3 times, K1, YO; rep from * to 11 sts before center st, ssk, K3, (K2tog, YO) twice, K2, YO, K1, YO, K2, (YO, ssk) twice, K3, K2tog, **YO, K1, (YO, ssk) 3 times, K3, K2tog; rep from ** to last 11 sts, YO, K1, (YO, ssk) 3 times, K1, YO, K3.

Row 9: K3, YO, K1, (K2tog, YO) 4 times, K1, *YO, ssk, K1, (K2tog, YO) 4 times, K1; rep from * to 11 sts before center st, YO, ssk, K1, (K2tog, YO) 3 times, K2, YO, K1, YO, K2, (YO, ssk) 3 times, K1, K2tog, YO, **K1, (YO, ssk) 4 times, K1, K2tog, YO; rep from ** to last 13 sts, K1, (YO, ssk) 4 times, K1, YO, K3.

Row 11: K3, YO, K1, (K2tog, YO) 5 times, *K1, YO, SK2P, YO, (K2tog, YO) 4 times; rep from * to 12 sts before center st, K1, YO, SK2P, YO, (K2tog, YO) 3 times, K2, YO, K1, YO, K2, (YO, ssk) 3 times, YO, SK2P, YO, K1,

**(YO, ssk) 4 times, YO, SK2P, YO, K1; rep from ** to last 14 sts, (YO, ssk) 5 times, K1, YO, K3.

Body of Shawl

Work tab CO (page 74) as foll: CO 3 sts. Knit 6 rows. Turn work 90° and pick up 3 sts along edge. Turn work 90° and pick up 3 sts from CO edge. (9 sts)

Row 1 (RS): K3, YO, K1, YO, K1 (center st), YO, K1, YO, K3. (13 sts)

Row 2 (WS): K3, purl to last 3 sts, K3.

Row 3: K3, YO, knit to center st, YO, K1, YO, knit to last 3 sts, YO, K3.

Work rows 2 and 3 another 40 times. Rep row 2 once more. (177 sts)

Lace Edging

Work charts as follows:

Chart A. (201 sts)

Chart B. (225 sts)

Chart A. (249 sts)

Chart C. (273 sts)

MAKE IT BIGGER!

With extra yarn, you can add additional repeats of charts A and B. Make sure to end with chart A before finishing the shawl with chart C.

Finishing

BO loosely purlwise as described on page 75. With tapestry needle, weave in ends. Using blocking wires or pins, block to finished measurements.

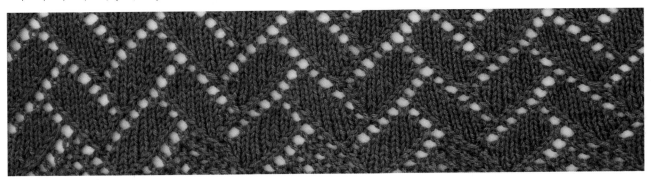

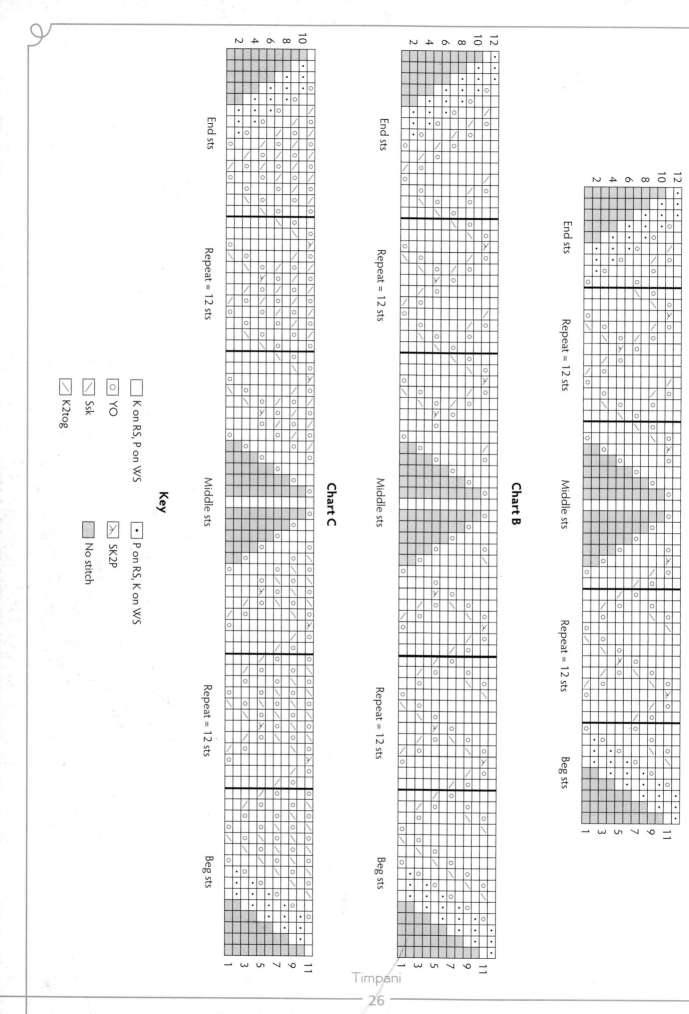

Key

	K on RS, P on WS		•	P on RS, K on WS
	YO		⋏	SK2P
	Ssk			No stitch
	K2tog			

Garter Love

There's something about garter stitch that just seems so cozy to me. It's probably one of the reasons I love it so much. This shawl is all about garter-stitch love! The simple body of the shawl transitions into the lace edge, where garter stitch is the star.

SKILL LEVEL: Intermediate ■■■□

FINISHED MEASUREMENTS: 52" x 20"

Materials

1 skein of Tosh Sock from Madelinetosh Hand-Dyed Yarns (100% superwash merino wool; 114 g; 395 yds) in color Cherry (**1**)

US size 4 (3.5 mm) circular needle, 24" or longer

4 stitch markers

Tapestry needle

Blocking wires and/or blocking pins

Gauge

18 sts and 32 rows = 4" in garter st

Lace Patterns

See charts A and B on page 30, or follow written instructions below.

Chart A

Row 1 (RS): YO, K1, *YO, ssk, K7, K2tog, YO, K1; rep from * to marker, YO.

Row 2 (WS): P1, *P3, K7, P2; rep from * to 2 sts before marker, P2.

Row 3: YO, K2, *K1, YO, ssk, K5, K2tog, YO, K2; rep from * to last st before marker, K1, YO.

Row 4: P2, *P4, K5, P3; rep from * to 3 sts before marker, P3.

Row 5: YO, K3, *K2, YO, ssk, K3, K2tog, YO, K3; rep from * to 2 sts before marker, K2, YO.

Row 6: P3, *P5, K3, P4; rep from * to 4 sts before marker, P4.

Row 7: YO, K4, *K3, YO, ssk, K1, K2tog, YO, K4; rep from * to 3 sts before marker, K3, YO.

Row 8: P4, *P6, K1, P5; rep from * to 5 sts before marker, P5.

Row 9: YO, K5, *K4, YO, SK2P, YO, K5; rep from * to 4 sts before marker, K4, YO.

Row 10: Purl all sts.

Row 11: YO, K6, *K3, K2tog, YO, K1, YO, ssk, K4; rep from * to 5 sts before marker, K5, YO.

Row 12: P3, K3, *K4, P5, K3; rep from * to 7 sts before marker, K4, P3.

Row 13: YO, K2, YO, ssk, K3, *K2, K2tog, YO, K3, YO, ssk, K3; rep from * to 6 sts before marker, K2, K2tog, YO, K2, YO.

Row 14: P5, K2, *K3, P7, K2; rep from * to 8 sts before marker, K3, P5.

Row 15: YO, K1, K2tog, YO, K1, YO, ssk, K2, *K1, K2tog, YO, K5, YO, ssk, K2; rep from * to 7 sts before marker, K1, K2tog, YO, K1, YO, ssk, K1, YO.

Row 16: P7, K1, *K2, P9, K1; rep from * to 9 sts before marker, K2, P7.

Row 17: YO, K1, YO, K2tog, YO, K3, YO, ssk, K1, *K2tog, YO, K7, YO, ssk, K1; rep from * to 8 sts before marker, K2tog, YO, K3, YO, ssk, YO, K1, YO.

Row 18: P10, *K1, P11; rep from * to 11 sts before marker, K1, P10.

Row 19: YO, K2, YO, K2tog, YO, K5, YO, SK2P, *YO, K9, YO, SK2P; rep from * to 9 sts before marker, YO, K5, YO, ssk, YO, K2, YO.

Row 20: Purl all sts.

Rep rows 1–20 for patt.

Chart B

Row 1 (RS): YO, K1, *YO, ssk, K7, K2tog, YO, K1; rep from * to marker, YO.

Row 2 (WS): P1, *P3, K7, P2; rep from * to 2 sts before marker, P2.

Row 3: YO, K2, *K1, YO, ssk, K5, K2tog, YO, K2; rep from * to last st before marker, K1, YO.

Row 4: P2, *P4, K5, P3; rep from * to 3 sts before marker, P3.

Row 5: YO, K2tog, YO, K1, *(YO, ssk) twice, K3, (K2tog, YO) twice, K1; rep from * to 2 sts before marker, YO, ssk, YO.

Row 6: P3, *P5, K3, P4; rep from * to 4 sts before marker, P4.

Row 7: YO, K2tog, YO, K2, *K1, (YO, ssk) twice, K1, (K2tog, YO) twice, K2; rep from * to 3 sts before marker, K1, YO, ssk, YO.

Row 8: P4, *P6, K1, P5; rep from * to 5 sts before marker, P5.

Row 9: YO, (K2tog, YO) twice, K1, *(YO, ssk) twice, YO, SK2P, YO, (K2tog, YO) twice, K1; rep from * to 4 sts before marker, (YO, ssk) twice, YO.

Body of Shawl

Work tab CO (page 74) as foll: CO 3 sts. Knit 6 rows. Turn work 90° and pick up 3 sts along edge. Turn work 90° and pick up 3 sts from CO edge. (9 sts)

Row 1 (RS): K3, PM, YO, K1, YO, PM, K1 (center st), PM, YO, K1, YO, PM, K3. (13 sts)

Row 2 (WS): Knit all sts (slipping markers).

Row 3: K3, SM, YO, knit to next marker, YO, SM, K1, SM, YO, knit to last 3 sts, YO, SM, K3.

Work rows 2 and 3 another 46 times. Rep row 2 once more. (201 sts)

Lace Edging

Cont working first 3 sts and last 3 sts in garter st (knit every row). Work the center st in St st (knit on RS, purl on WS). Work chart A between st markers on each half of shawl. (249 sts)

Work chart B between st markers on each half of shawl. (269 sts)

MAKE IT BIGGER!

With extra yarn, you can add as many repeats of chart A as you like before working chart B.

Finishing

BO loosely purlwise as described on page 75. With tapestry needle, weave in ends. Using blocking wires or pins, block to finished measurements.

Chart A

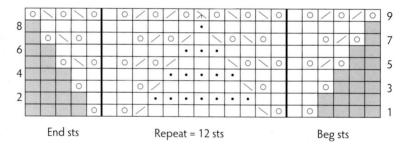

End sts   Repeat = 12 sts   Beg sts

Chart B

End sts   Repeat = 12 sts   Beg sts

Key

○ YO	• P on RS, K on WS
☐ K on RS, P on WS	⋋ SK2P
╲ Ssk	▨ No stitch
╱ K2tog	

Allover-Lace Shawls

The shawls in this section feature allover-lace patterns. Some shawls are extremely simple, while others involve several lace motifs that flow into one another. Whether you love the challenge of tackling a large lace chart or are just looking for a quick, easy lace project, there is a project for you in this section.

Over the Moon

Wrap yourself in this warm alpaca-blend shawl on a moonlit walk. Stroll through the neighborhood with your partner or sneak into the woods looking for werewolves—you're bound to turn heads with this one.

Materials

1 skein of Alpaca Sox from Classic Elite Yarns (60% alpaca, 20% merino wool, 20% nylon; 100 g; 450 yds) in color 1807 Verdis 〔**1**〕

US size 4 (3.5 mm) circular needle, 24" or longer

Tapestry needle

Blocking wires and/or blocking pins

Gauge

22 sts and 32 rows = 4" in St st

Lace Patterns

See charts A, B, C, and D on page 36, or follow written instructions below.

Chart A

Row 1 (RS): K3, YO, *K1, K2tog, YO, K1, YO, ssk, K2; rep from * to 3 sts before center st, K3, YO, K1, YO, K3, **K2, K2tog, YO, K1, YO, ssk, K1; rep from ** to last 3 sts, YO, K3.

Row 2 and all even-numbered rows (WS): K3, purl to last 3 sts, K3.

Row 3: K3, YO, K1, *K2tog, YO, K3, YO, ssk, K1; rep from * to 4 sts before center st, K4, YO, K1, YO, K4, **K1, K2tog, YO, K3, YO, ssk; rep from ** to last 4 sts, K1, YO, K3.

Row 5: K3, YO, K1, K2tog, *YO, K5, YO, SK2P; rep from * to 4 sts before center st, YO, K4, YO, K1, YO, K4, YO, **SK2P, YO, K5, YO; rep from ** to last 6 sts, ssk, K1, YO, K3.

Row 7: K3, YO, K2, K2tog, *YO, K5, YO, CDD; rep from * to 5 sts before center st, YO, K5, YO, K1, YO, K5, YO, **CDD, YO, K5, YO; rep from ** to last 7 sts, ssk, K2, YO, K3.

Row 9: K3, YO, K3, K2tog, *YO, K5, YO, CDD; rep from * to 6 sts before center st, YO, K6, YO, K1, YO, K6, YO, **CDD, YO, K5, YO; rep from ** to last 8 sts, ssk, K3, YO, K3.

Row 10: K3, purl to last 3 sts, K3.

Chart B

Row 1 (RS): K3, YO, K1, K2tog, YO, K2, *K1, YO, ssk, K1, K2tog, YO, K2; rep from * to center st, YO, K1, YO, **K2, YO, ssk, K1, K2tog, YO, K1; rep from ** to last 8 sts, K2, YO, ssk, K1, YO, K3.

Row 2 and all even-numbered rows (WS): K3, purl to last 3 sts, K3.

Row 3: K3, YO, K1, K2tog, YO, K3, *K2, YO, SK2P, YO, K3; rep from * to 1 st before center st, (K1, YO) twice, K1, **K3, YO, SK2P, YO, K2; rep from ** to last 9 sts, K3, YO, ssk, K1, YO, K3.

Row 5: K3, YO, K4, K2tog, YO, K1, *YO, ssk, K3, K2tog, YO, K1; rep from * to 2 sts before center st, K2, YO, K1, YO, K2, **K1, YO, ssk, K3, K2tog, YO; rep from ** to last 10 sts, K1, YO, ssk, K4, YO, K3.

Row 7: K3, YO, K1, YO, ssk, K1, K2tog, YO, K2, *K1, YO, ssk, K1, K2tog, YO, K2; rep from * to 3 sts before center st, K3, YO, K1, YO, K3, **K2, YO, ssk, K1, K2tog, YO, K1; rep from ** to last 11 sts, K2, YO, ssk, K1, K2tog, YO, K1, YO, K3.

Row 8: K3, purl to last 3 sts, K3.

Chart C

Row 1 (RS): K3, YO, K1, *K2, YO, SK2P, YO, K3; rep from * to 4 sts before center st, K4, YO, K1, YO, K4, **K3, YO, SK2P, YO, K2; rep from ** to last 4 sts, K1, YO, K3.

Row 2 and all even numbered rows (WS): K3, purl to last 3 sts, K3.

Row 3: K3, YO, K2, *K2, YO, CDD, YO, K3; rep from * to 5 sts before center st, K5, YO, K1, YO, K5, **K3, YO, CDD, YO, K2; rep from ** to last 5 sts, K2, YO, K3.

Row 5: K3, YO, K3, *K2, YO, CDD, YO, K3; rep from * to 6 sts before center st, K2, YO, K2tog, YO, K2, YO, K1, YO, K2, YO, ssk, YO, K2, **K3, YO, CDD, YO, K2; rep from ** to last 6 sts, K3, YO, K3.

Row 7: K3, YO, K1, YO, K2tog, YO, K1, *K2tog, YO, K3, YO, ssk, K1; rep from * to 8 sts before center st, K2tog, YO, K3, YO, ssk, (K1, YO) twice, K1, K2tog, YO, K3, YO,

ssk, **K1, K2tog, YO, K3, YO, ssk; rep from ** to last 7 sts, K1, YO, ssk, YO, K1, YO, K3.

Row 9: K3, YO, K1, YO, K2tog, YO, K1, YO, SK2P, *YO, K5, YO, SK2P; rep from * to 8 sts before center st, YO, K1, YO, K2tog, YO, K1, YO, ssk, K2, YO, K1, YO, K2, K2tog, YO, K1, YO, ssk, YO, K1, YO, **SK2P, YO, K5, YO; rep from ** to last 10 sts, SK2P, YO, K1, YO, ssk, YO, K1, YO, K3.

Row 10: K3, purl to last 3 sts, K3.

Chart D

Row 1 (RS): K3, YO, *K1, K2tog, YO, K1, YO, ssk, K2; rep from * to 3 sts before center st, K3, YO, K1, YO, K3, **K2, K2tog, YO, K1, YO, ssk, K1; rep from ** to last 3 sts, YO, K3.

Row 2 and all even-numbered rows (WS): K3, purl to last 3 sts, K3.

Row 3: K3, YO, K1, *K2tog, YO, K3, YO, ssk, K1; rep from * to 4 sts before center st, K4, YO, K1, YO, K4, **K1, K2tog, YO, K3, YO, ssk; rep from ** to last 4 sts, K1, YO, K3.

Row 5: K3, YO, K1, K2tog, *YO, K1, YO, SK2P; rep from * to 4 sts before center st, YO, K4, YO, K1, YO, K4, YO, **SK2P, YO, K1, YO; rep from ** to last 6 sts, ssk, K1, YO, K3.

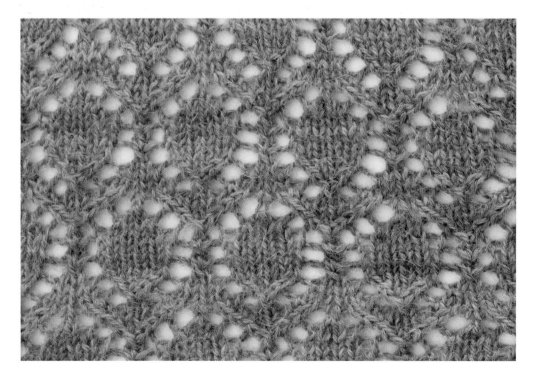

Row 7: K3, YO, K2, K2tog, *YO, K1, YO, CDD; rep from * to 5 sts before center st, YO, K1, YO, ssk, YO, K2, YO, K1, YO, K2, YO, K2tog, YO, K1, YO, **CDD, YO, K1, YO; rep from ** to last 7 sts, ssk, K2, YO, K3.

Row 9: K3, YO, K3, K2tog, *YO, K1, YO, CDD; rep from * to 3 sts before center st, YO, K3, YO, K1, YO, K3, YO, **CDD, YO, K1, YO; rep from ** to last 8 sts, ssk, K3, YO, K3.

Row 11: K3, YO, K4, K2tog, *YO, K1, YO, CDD; rep from * to 4 sts before center st, YO, K4, YO, K1, YO, K4, YO, **CDD, YO, K1, YO; rep from ** to last 9 sts, ssk, K4, YO, K3.

Row 13: K3, YO, K2, YO, K2tog, YO, K1, K2tog, *YO, K1, YO, CDD; rep from * to 5 sts before center st, YO, K5, YO, K1, YO, K5, YO, **CDD, YO, K1, YO; rep from ** to last 10 sts, ssk, K1, YO, ssk, YO, K2, YO, K3.

Row 14: K3, purl to last 3 sts, K3.

Set-Up Rows

Work tab CO (page 74) as foll: CO 3 sts. Knit 6 rows. Turn work 90° and pick up 3 sts along edge. Turn work 90° and pick up 3 sts from CO edge. (9 sts)

Row 1 (RS): K3, YO, K1, YO, K1 (center st), YO, K1, YO, K3. (13 sts)

Row 2 (WS): K3, purl to last 3 sts, K3.

Row 3: K3, YO, knit to center st, YO, K1, YO, knit to last 3 sts, YO, K3.

Work rows 2 and 3 another 3 times. Rep row 2 once more. (29 sts)

Body of Shawl

Work charts A, B, and C four times total.

Stitch Count	
First rep of charts A, B, and C	93 sts
Second rep of charts A, B, and C	157 sts
Third rep of charts A, B, and C	221 sts
Fourth rep of charts A, B, and C	285 sts

MAKE IT BIGGER!

If you have a second skein of yarn, add additional repeats of charts A, B, and C before moving on to chart D.

Lace Edging

Work rows 1–13 of chart D. (317 sts)

MAKE IT BIGGER!

If you still have more than a third of a skein of yarn left, you can work rows 1–14 of chart D, and then work rows 1–13 of chart D once more before binding off.

Finishing

BO loosely purlwise as described on page 75. With tapestry needle, weave in ends. Using blocking wires or pins, block to finished measurements.

Chart A

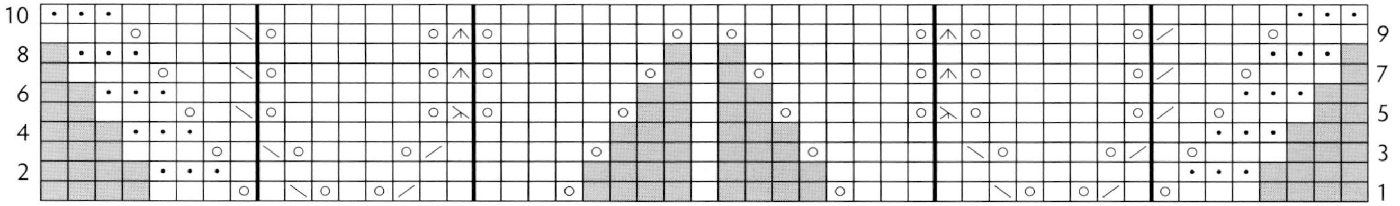

End sts

Repeat = 8 sts

Middle sts

Repeat = 8 sts

Beg sts

Row numbers: 10, 8, 6, 4, 2 (left side, top); 1, 3, 5, 7, 9 (bottom)

Chart B

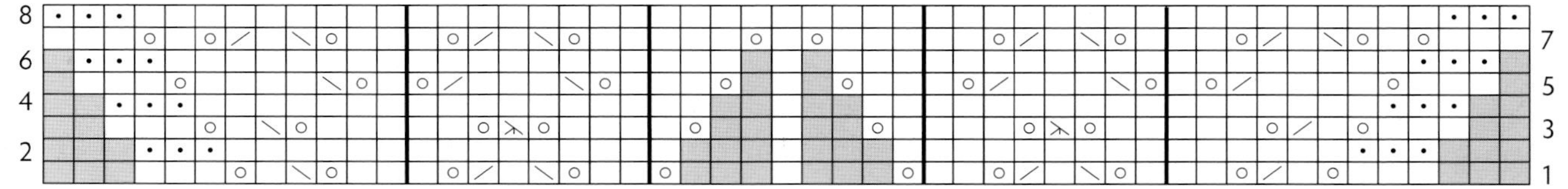

End sts

Repeat = 8 sts

Middle sts

Repeat = 8 sts

Beg sts

Row numbers: 8, 6, 4, 2 (top); 1, 3, 5, 7 (bottom)

Chart C

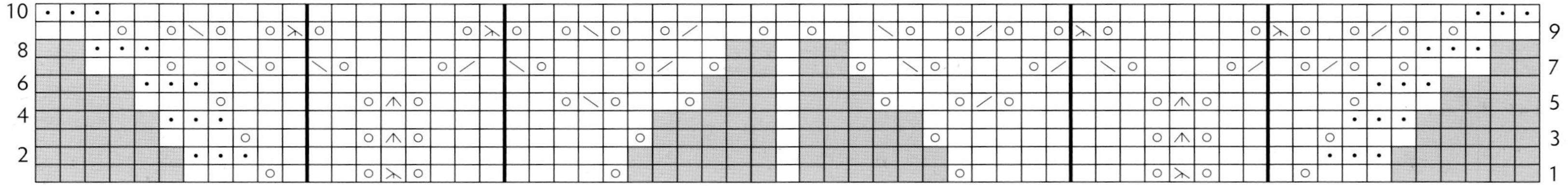

End sts

Repeat = 8 sts

Middle sts

Repeat = 8 sts

Beg sts

Row numbers: 10, 8, 6, 4, 2 (top); 1, 3, 5, 7, 9 (bottom)

Chart D

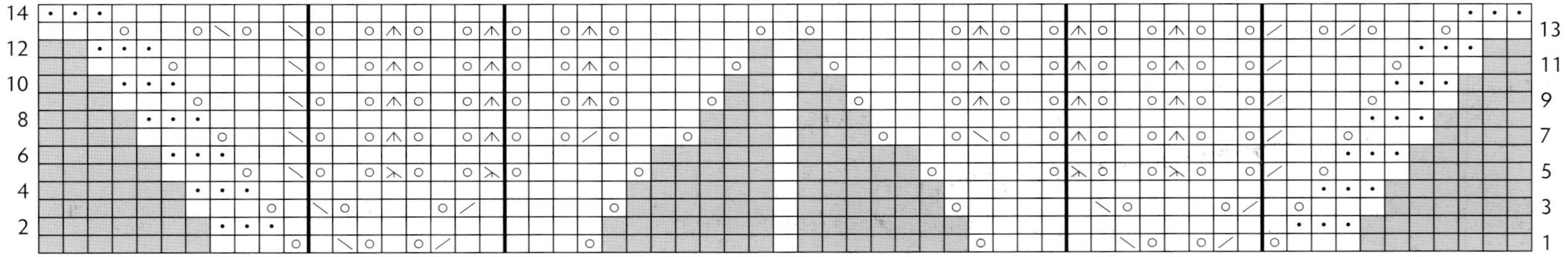

End sts

Repeat = 8 sts

Middle sts

Repeat = 8 sts

Beg sts

Row numbers: 14, 12, 10, 8, 6, 4, 2 (top); 1, 3, 5, 7, 9, 11, 13 (bottom)

Key

☐	K on RS, P on WS
•	P on RS, K on WS
⋏	SK2P
○	YO
⋏	CDD
/	K2tog
\	Ssk
▦	No stitch

Happenstance

The lace on this shawl seems to twist and turn its way to the edge. The combination of knit and purl stitches results in a shawl that is delicate and textured at the same time.

FINISHED MEASUREMENTS: 48" x 20"

Materials

1 skein of Artisan Sock from Hazel Knits (90% superwash merino wool, 10% nylon; 100 g; 400 yds) in color 217 Laguna

US size 4 (3.5 mm) circular needle, 24" or longer

4 stitch markers

Tapestry needle

Blocking wires and/or blocking pins

Gauge

20 sts and 32 rows = 4" in St st

Lace Patterns

See charts A and B on page 41, or follow written instructions below.

Chart A

Row 1 (RS): YO, *P1, K1, YO, ssk, P1, K4, P1, K2tog, YO, K1, P1; rep from * to end, YO.

Row 2 (WS): P1, *K1, P3, K1, P4, K1, P3, K1; rep from * to 1 st before marker, P1.

Row 3: YO, P1, *P1, K2, YO, ssk, P1, K2, P1, K2tog, YO, K2, P1; rep from * to 1 st before marker, P1, YO.

Row 4: P1, K1, *K1, P4, K1, P2, K1, P4, K1; rep from * to 2 sts before marker, K1, P1.

Row 5: YO, K1, P1, *P1, K3, YO, ssk, P2, K2tog, YO, K3, P1; rep from * to 2 sts before marker, P1, K1, YO.

Row 6: P2, K1, *K1, P5, K1; rep from * to 3 sts before marker, K1, P2.

Row 7: YO, K2tog, YO, P1, *P1, YO, ssk, K3, P2, K3, K2tog, YO, P1; rep from * to 3 sts before marker, P1, YO, ssk, YO.

Row 8: P2, K2, *K2, (P4, K2) twice; rep from * to 4 sts before marker, K2, P2.

Row 9: YO, K2tog, YO, P1, K1, *K1, P1, YO, ssk, K2, P2, K2, K2tog, YO, P1, K1; rep from * to 4 sts before marker, K1, P1, YO, ssk, YO.

Row 10: P2, K2, P1, *P1, (K2, P3) twice, K2, P1; rep from * to 5 sts before marker, P1, K2, P2.

Row 11: YO, K2tog, YO, P1, K2, *K2, P1, YO, ssk, K1, P2, K1, K2tog, YO, P1, K2; rep from * to 5 sts before marker, K2, P1, YO, ssk, YO.

Row 12: P2, K2, P2, *P2, (K2, P2) 3 times; rep from * to 6 sts before marker, P2, K2, P2.

Row 13: YO, K2tog, YO, P1, K3, *K3, P1, YO, ssk, P2, K2tog, YO, P1, K3; rep from * to 6 sts before marker, K3, P1, YO, ssk, YO.

Row 14: P2, K3, P2, *P2, K3, P1, K2, P1, K3, P2; rep from * to 7 sts before marker, P2, K3, P2.

Row 15: YO, P1, K1, YO, ssk, P1, K2, *K2, P1, K2tog, YO, K1, P2, K1, YO, ssk, P1, K2; rep from * to 7 sts before marker, K2, P1, K2tog, YO, K1, P1, YO.

Row 16: K2, P3, K2, P1, *P1, (K2, P3) twice, K2, P1; rep from * to 8 sts before marker, P1, K2, P3, K2.

Row 17: YO, P2, K2, YO, ssk, P1, K1, *K1, P1, K2tog, YO, K2, P2, K2, YO, ssk, P1, K1; rep from * to 8 sts before marker, K1, P1, K2tog, YO, K2, P2, YO.

Row 18: P1, K2, P4, K2, *K2, (P4, K2) twice; rep from * to 9 sts before marker, K2, P4, K2, P1.

Row 19: YO, K1, P2, K3, YO, ssk, P1, *P1, K2tog, YO, K3, P2, K3, YO, ssk, P1; rep from * to 9 sts before marker, P1, K2tog, YO, K3, P2, K1, YO.

Row 20: P2, K2, P5, K1, *K1, P5, K1; rep from * to 10 sts before marker, K1, P5, K2, P2.

Row 21: YO, K2tog, YO, P2, YO, ssk, K3, P1, *P1, K3, K2tog, YO, P2, YO, ssk, K3, P1; rep from * to 10 sts before marker, P1, K3, K2tog, YO, P2, YO, ssk, YO.

Row 22: P2, K4, P4, K1, *K1, P4, K4, P4, K1; rep from * to 11 sts before marker, K1, P4, K4, P2.

Row 23: YO, K2tog, YO, P1, K2, P1, YO, ssk, K2, P1, *P1, K2, K2tog, YO, P1, K2, P1, YO, ssk, K2, P1; rep from * to 11 sts before marker, P1, K2, K2tog, YO, P1, K2, P1, YO, ssk, YO.

Row 24: (P2, K2) twice, P3, K1, *K1, P3, K2, P2, K2, P3, K1; rep from * to 12 sts before marker, K1, P3, (K2, P2) twice.

Row 25: YO, K2tog, YO, P1, K4, P1, YO, ssk, K1, P1, *P1, K1, K2tog, YO, P1, K4, P1, YO, ssk, K1, P1; rep from * to last 12 sts, P1, K1, K2tog, YO, P1, K4, P1, YO, ssk, YO.

Row 26: P2, K2, P4, K2, P2, K1, *K1, P2, K2, P4, K2, P2, K1; rep from * to 13 sts before marker, K1, P2, K2, P4, K2, P2.

Row 27: YO, K2tog, YO, P1, K6, P1, YO, ssk, P1, *P1, K2tog, YO, P1, K6, P1, YO, ssk, P1; rep from * to 13 sts before marker, P1, K2tog, YO, P1, K6, P1, YO, ssk, YO.

Row 28: P3, K1, P6, K1, P2, K1, *K1, P2, K1, P6, K1, P2, K1; rep from * to 14 sts before marker, K1, P2, K1, P6, K1, P3.

Rep rows 1–28 for patt.

Chart B

Row 1 (RS): YO, P1, K1, YO, ssk, P1, K2, *K2, P1, K2tog, YO, K1, P2, K1, YO, ssk, P1, K2; rep from * to 7 sts before marker, K2, P1, K2tog, YO, K1, P1, YO.

Row 2 (WS): K2, P3, K2, P1, *P1, (K2, P3) twice, K2, P1; rep from * to 8 sts before marker, P1, K2, P3, K2.

Row 3: YO, P2, (YO, ssk) twice, P1, K1, *K1, P1, (K2tog, YO) twice, P2, (YO, ssk) twice, P1, K1; rep from * to 8 sts before marker, K1, P1, (K2tog, YO) twice, P2, YO.

Row 4: P1, K2, P4, K2, *K2, (P4, K2) twice; rep from * to 9 sts before marker, K2, P4, K2, P1.

Row 5: YO, K1, P2, K1, (YO, ssk) twice, P1, *P1, (K2tog, YO) twice, K1, P2, K1, (YO, ssk) twice, P1; rep from * to 9 sts before marker, P1, (K2tog, YO) twice, K1, P2, K1, YO.

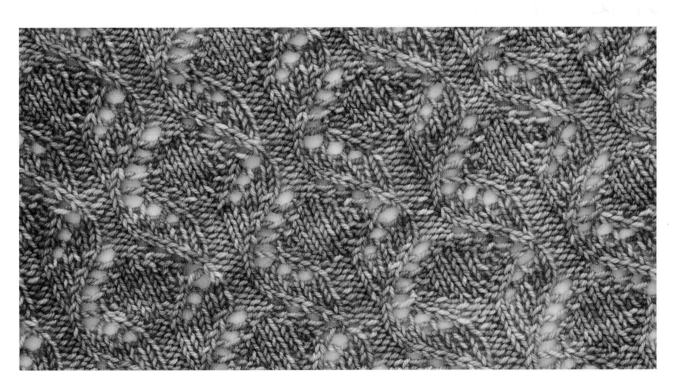

Row 6: P2, K2, P5, K1, *K1, P5, K1; rep from * to 10 sts before marker, K1, P5, K2, P2.

Row 7: YO, K2tog, YO, P2, (YO, ssk) twice, K1, P1, *P1, K1, (K2tog, YO) twice, P2, (YO, ssk) twice, K1, P1; rep from * to 10 sts before marker, P1, K1, (K2tog, YO) twice, P2, YO, ssk, YO.

Row 8: P2, K4, P4, K1, *K1, P4, K4, P4, K1; rep from * to 11 sts before marker, K1, P4, K4, P2.

Row 9: YO, K2tog, YO, P1, K2, P1, (YO, ssk) twice, P1, *P1, (K2tog, YO) twice, P1, K2, P1, (YO, ssk) twice, P1; rep from * to 11 sts before marker, P1, (K2tog, YO) twice, P1, K2, P1, YO, ssk, YO.

Row 10: (P2, K2) twice, P3, K1, *K1, P3, K2, P2, K2, P3, K1; rep from * to 12 sts before marker, K1, P3, (K2, P2) twice.

Row 11: YO, K2tog, YO, P1, K4, P1, YO, ssk, K1, P1, *P1, K1, K2tog, YO, P1, K4, P1, YO, ssk, K1, P1; rep from * to last 12 sts, P1, K1, K2tog, YO, P1, K4, P1, YO, ssk, YO.

Row 12: P2, K2, P4, K2, P2, K1, *K1, P2, K2, P4, K2, P2, K1; rep from * to 13 sts before marker, K1, P2, K2, P4, K2, P2.

Row 13: YO, K2tog, YO, P1, K6, P1, YO, ssk, P1, *P1, K2tog, YO, P1, K6, P1, YO, ssk, P1; rep from * to 13 sts before marker, P1, K2tog, YO, P1, K6, P1, YO, ssk, YO.

Row 14: P3, K1, P6, K1, P2, K1, *K1, P2, K1, P6, K1, P2, K1; rep from * to 14 sts before marker, K1, P2, K1, P6, K1, P3.

Set-Up Rows

Work tab CO (page 74) as foll: CO 3 sts. Knit 6 rows. Turn work 90° and pick up 3 sts along edge. Turn work 90° and pick up 3 sts from CO edge. (9 sts)

Row 1 (RS): K2, PM, YO, K2, YO, PM, K1 (center st), PM, YO, K2, YO, PM, K2. (13 sts)

Row 2 (WS): K2, purl to last 2 sts (slipping markers), K2.

Row 3: K1, *K1, SM, YO, K1, P2, K1, YO, SM; rep from * to last 2 sts, K2. (17 sts)

Row 4: K2, SM, P2, K2, P2, SM, P1, SM, P2, K2, P2, SM, K2.

Row 5: K1, *K1, SM, YO, K2, P2, K2, YO, SM; rep from * to last 2 sts, K2. (21 sts)

Row 6: K2, SM, P3, K2, P3, SM, P1, SM, P3, K2, P3, SM, K2.

Row 7: K1, *K1, SM, YO, K2tog, YO, P1, K2, P1, YO, ssk, YO, SM; rep from * to last 2 sts, K2. (25 sts)

Row 8: K2, SM, P3, K1, P2, K1, P3, SM, P1, SM, P3, K1, P2, K1, P3, SM, K2.

Row 9: K1, *K1, SM, YO, K2tog, YO, P1, K4, P1, YO, ssk, YO, SM; rep from * to last 2 sts, K2. (29 sts)

Row 10: K2, SM, P3, K1, P4, K1, P3, SM, P1, SM, P3, K1, P4, K1, P3, SM, K2.

Row 11: K1, *K1, SM, YO, K2tog, YO, P1, K6, P1, YO, ssk, YO, SM; rep from * to last 2 sts, K2. (33 sts)

Row 12: K2, SM, P3, K1, P6, K1, P3, SM, P1, SM, P3, K1, P6, K1, P3, SM, K2.

Body of Shawl

Cont working first 2 sts and last 2 sts in garter st (knit every row), and center st in St st (knit on RS, purl on WS). Work chart A between st markers on each half of shawl 3 times total. Work rows 1–14 of chart A once more between stitch markers on each half of shawl.

Stitch count	
First rep of chart A	89 sts
Second rep of chart A	145 sts
Third rep of chart A	201 sts
Fourth rep of chart A, rows 1–14 only	229 sts

MAKE IT BIGGER!

If you have a second skein available, you can add additional repeats of chart A, making sure to work only rows 1–14 of chart A on the last repeat before moving on to chart B.

Lace Edging

Work chart B between st markers on each half of shawl. (257 sts)

Finishing

BO loosely knitwise as described on page 75. With tapestry needle, weave in ends. Using blocking wires or pins, block to finished measurements.

Chart A

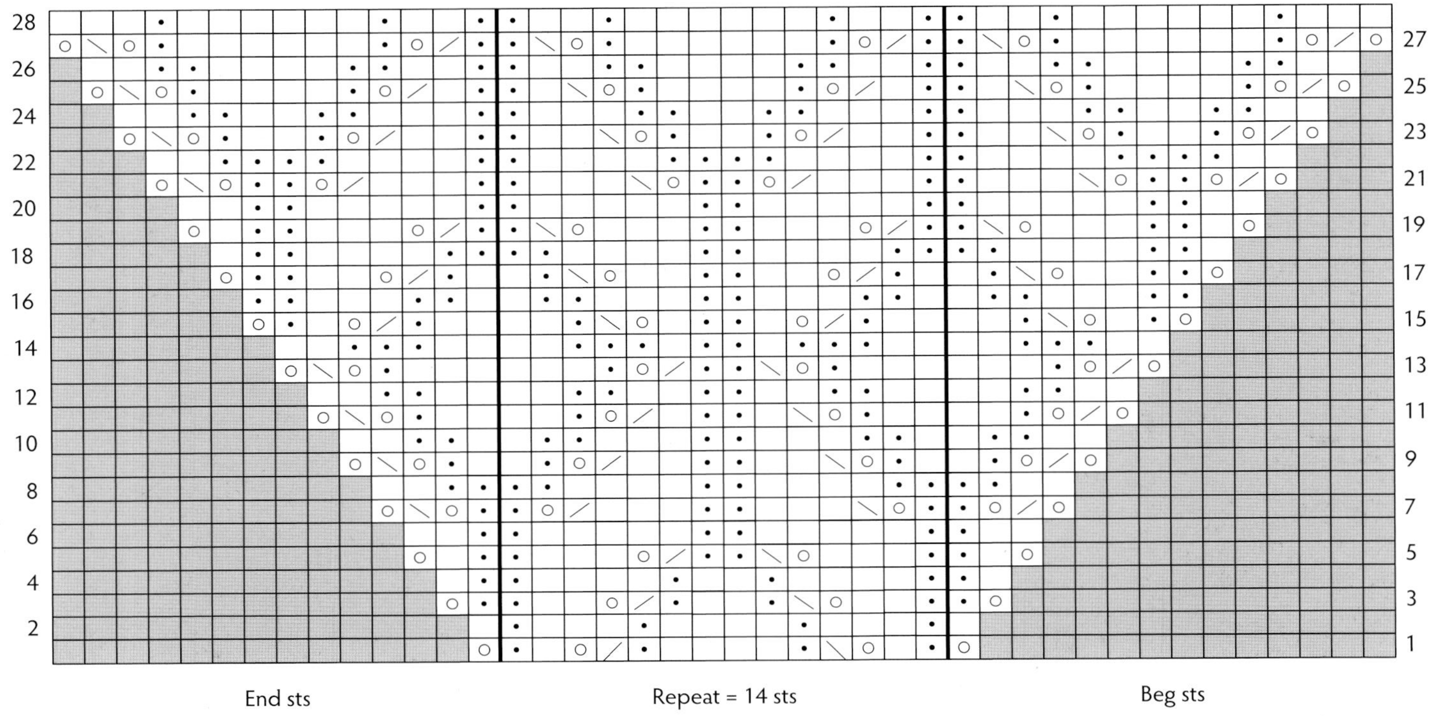

27 25 23 21 19 17 15 13 11 9 7 5 3 1

Beg sts

Repeat = 14 sts

End sts

28 26 24 22 20 18 16 14 12 10 8 6 4 2

Chart B

13 11 9 7 5 3 1

Beg sts

Repeat = 14 sts

End sts

14 12 10 8 6 4 2

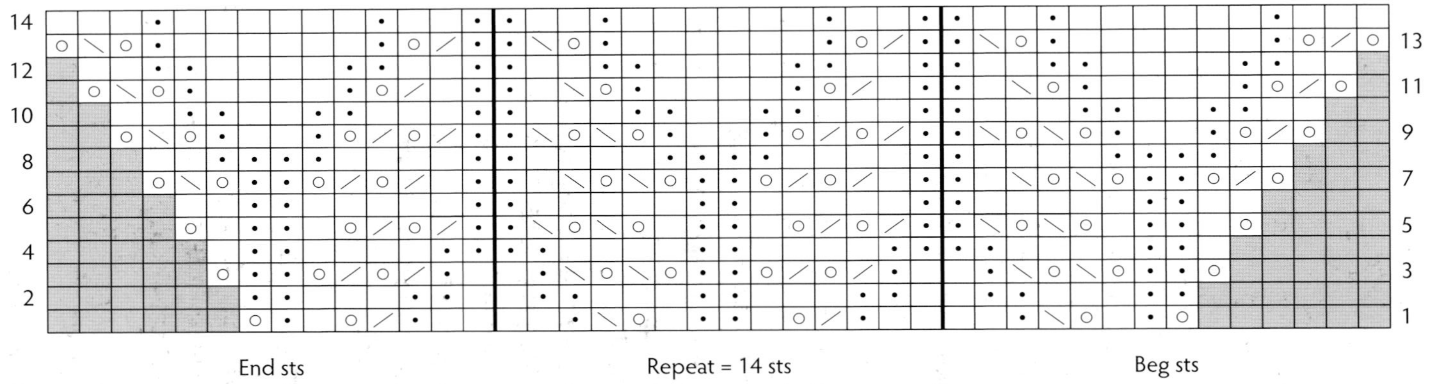

Key

⊙	YO
•	P on RS, K on WS
☐	K on RS, P on WS
／	Ssk
＼	K2tog
▨	No stitch

Francolin

The kite-like lace motif makes me
want to wear this shawl outside on
a windy morning to see where it
might take me. This shawl is going
to make you take flight!

SKILL LEVEL: Intermediate ●●■◻

FINISHED MEASUREMENTS: 60" x 28"

Materials

2 skeins of Spud & Chloë Fine Sock from Blue Sky Alpacas (80% wool, 20% silk; 65 g; 248 yds) in color 7814 Shitake (**1**)

US size 5 (3.75 mm) circular needle, 24" or longer

4 stitch markers

Tapestry needle

Blocking wires and/or blocking pins

Gauge

16 sts and 22 rows = 4" in St st

Lace Patterns

See charts A, B, and C on page 46, or follow written instructions below.

Chart A

Row 1 (RS): YO, *K3, YO, SK2P, YO, K2; rep from * to 1 st before marker, K1, YO.

Row 2 and all even-numbered rows (WS): Purl all sts.

Row 3: YO, K1, *K3, YO, SK2P, YO, K2; rep from * to 2 sts before marker, K2, YO.

Row 5: YO, K2, *K3, YO, SK2P, YO, K2; rep from * to 3 sts before marker, K3, YO.

Row 7: YO, K3, *K2, K2tog, YO, K1, YO, ssk, K1; rep from * to 4 sts before marker, K4, YO.

Row 9: YO, K2, YO, ssk, *K1, K2tog, YO, K3, YO, ssk; rep from * to 5 sts before marker, K1, K2tog, YO, K2, YO.

Row 11: YO, K1, YO, K2tog, YO, K1, YO, *SK2P, YO, K5, YO; rep from * to 7 sts before marker, SK2P, YO, K1, YO, ssk, YO, K1, YO.

Row 13: YO, ssk, YO, K3, YO, K2tog, *K1, ssk, YO, K3, YO, K2tog; rep from * to 8 sts before marker, K1, ssk, YO, K3, YO, K2tog, YO.

Row 15: YO, K2, YO, ssk, YO, K1, YO, K2tog, K1, *K2, ssk, YO, K1, YO, K2tog, K1; rep from * to 9 sts before marker, K2, ssk, YO, K1, YO, K2tog, YO, K2, YO.

Row 17: YO, K2, YO, K2tog, YO, K1, YO, SK2P, YO, K2, *K3, YO, SK2P, YO, K2; rep from * to 11 sts before marker, K3, YO, SK2P, YO, K1, YO, ssk, YO, K2, YO.

Row 19: YO, K4, YO, K2tog, YO, K1, YO, SK2P, YO, K2, *K3, YO, SK2P, YO, K2; rep from * to 13 sts before marker, K3, YO, SK2P, YO, K1, YO, ssk, YO, K4, YO.

Row 21: YO, K2, YO, K2tog, YO, K2, *K3, YO, SK2P, YO, K2; rep from * to 7 sts before marker, K3, YO, ssk, YO, K2, YO.

Row 22: Purl all sts.

Rep rows 1–22 for patt.

Chart B

Row 1 (RS): YO, *K3, YO, SK2P, YO, K2; rep from * to 1 st before marker, K1, YO.

Row 2 and all even-numbered rows (WS): Purl all sts.

Row 3: YO, K1, *K2, K2tog, YO, K1, YO, ssk, K1; rep from * to 2 sts before marker, K2, YO.

Row 5: YO, K2, *K1, K2tog, YO, K3, YO, ssk; rep from * to 3 sts before marker, K3, YO.

Row 7: YO, K2, YO, *SK2P, YO, K5, YO; rep from * to 5 sts before marker, SK2P, YO, K2, YO.

Row 9: (YO, K1) twice, YO, K2tog, *K1, ssk, YO, K3, YO, K2tog; rep from * to 5 sts before marker, K1, ssk, (YO, K1) twice, YO.

Row 11: YO, K2, YO, K1, YO, K2tog, K1, *K2, ssk, YO, K1, YO, K2tog, K1; rep from * to 7 sts before marker, K2, ssk, YO, K1, YO, K2, YO.

Row 12: Purl all sts.

Rep rows 1–12 for patt.

Chart C

Row 1 (RS): YO, *K1, YO, K2, SK2P, YO, K2; rep from * to 1 st before marker, K1, YO.

Row 2 and all even-numbered rows (WS): Purl all sts.

Row 3: YO, K1, *YO, K3, SK2P, K1, YO, K1; rep from * to 2 sts before marker, K2, YO.

Row 5: YO, K2, *K3, YO, SK2P, K2, YO; rep from * to 3 sts before marker, K3, YO.

Row 7: YO, K3, *YO, K1, YO, K1, SK2P, K3; rep from * to 4 sts before marker, K4, YO.

Row 9: YO, K2tog, YO, K2, *K1, YO, K2, SK2P, YO, K2; rep from * to 5 sts before marker, K1, YO, K2, K2tog, YO.

Row 11: YO, K1, K2tog, K1, YO, K1, *YO, K3, SK2P, K1, YO, K1; rep from * to 6 sts before marker, YO, K3, K2tog, K1, YO.

Row 13: YO, K1, YO, SK2P, K2, YO, *K3, YO, SK2P, K2, YO; rep from * to 7 sts before marker, K3, YO, K2tog, K2, YO.

Francolin

Row 15: (YO, K1) twice, K2tog, K3, *(YO, K1) twice, SK2P, K3; rep from * to 8 sts before marker, (YO, K1) twice, SK2P, K3, YO.

Row 16: Purl all sts.

Set-Up Rows

Work tab CO (page 74) as foll: CO 3 sts. Knit 6 rows. Turn work 90° and pick up 3 sts along edge. Turn work 90° and pick up 3 sts from CO edge. (9 sts)

Row 1 (RS): K3, PM, YO, K1, YO, PM, K1 (center st), PM, YO, K1, YO, PM, K3. (13 sts)

Row 2 (WS): K3, purl to last 3 sts (slipping markers), K3.

Row 3: K3, SM, YO, knit to next marker, YO, SM, K1, SM, YO, knit to last 3 sts, YO, SM, K3.

Work rows 2 and 3 twice more. Rep row 2 once more. (25 sts)

Body of Shawl

Cont working first 3 sts and last 3 sts in garter st (knit every row), and working the center st in St st (knit on RS, purl on WS). Work chart A between st markers on each half of shawl 3 times total.

Stitch Count	
First rep of chart A	89 sts
Second rep of chart A	153 sts
Third rep of chart A	217 sts

Work chart B between st markers on each half of shawl twice.

Stitch Count	
First rep of chart B	249 sts
Second rep of chart B	281 sts

MAKE IT BIGGER!

There are lots of options to make this shawl larger if you have extra yarn. Any of the charts can be repeated to add length to your shawl.

Lace Edging

Work chart C between st markers on each half of shawl. (313 sts)

Finishing

BO loosely knitwise as described on page 75. With tapestry needle, weave in ends. Using blocking wires or pins, block to finished measurements.

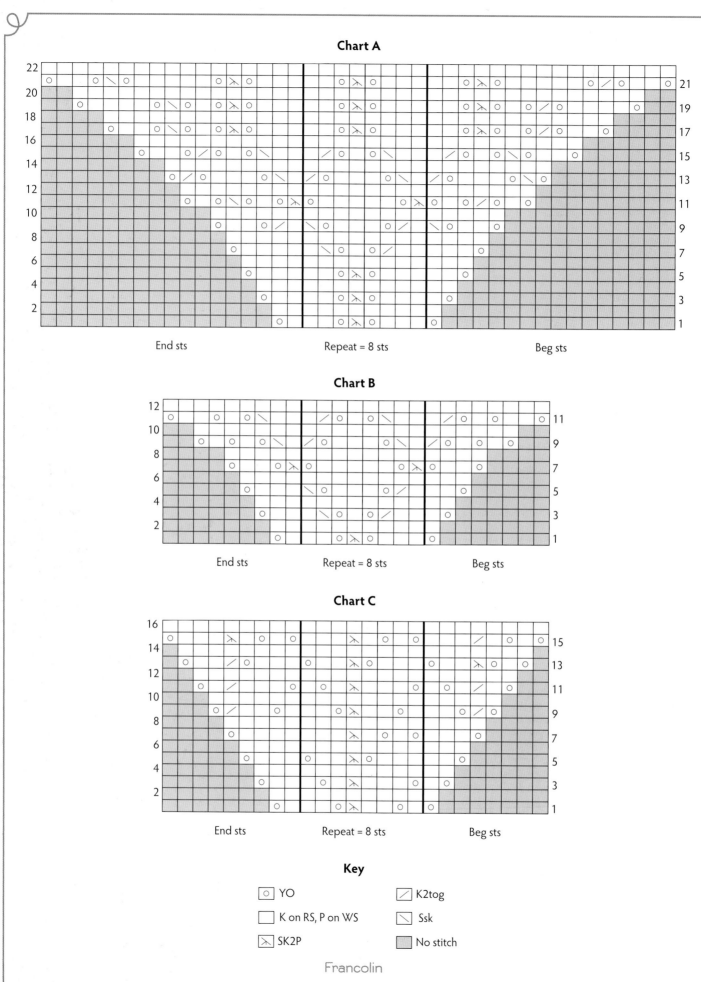

Chart A

End sts

Repeat = 8 sts

Beg sts

Chart B

End sts

Repeat = 8 sts

Beg sts

Chart C

End sts

Repeat = 8 sts

Beg sts

Key

⊙ YO		╱ K2tog	
☐ K on RS, P on WS		╲ Ssk	
⋏ SK2P		▨ No stitch	

Francolin

Herbstwald

Herbstwald means "autumn forest" in German. And this shawl looks like it could be found right on the forest floor. With leaf motifs throughout the shawl, transitioning from one to another, it calls to mind thoughts of a crisp fall day. All you need is some apple cider and hand-knit socks, and you'll be ready for October.

SKILL LEVEL: Intermediate

FINISHED MEASUREMENTS: 64" x 26"

Materials

2 skeins of Sock-a-Licious from Kolláge Yarns (70% fine superwash merino wool, 10% mulberry silk, 20% nylon; 100 g; 354 yds) in color 7801 Mango **1**

US size 3 (3.25 mm) circular needle, 24" or longer

4 stitch markers

Tapestry needle

Blocking wires and/or blocking pins

Gauge

20 sts and 40 rows = 4" in St st

Lace Patterns

See chart A on page 50 and charts B and C on page 51, or follow written instructions below.

Chart A

Row 1 (RS): YO, *K4, K2tog, YO, K1, YO, ssk, K3; rep from * to 1 st before marker, K1, YO.

Row 2 and all even-numbered rows (WS): Purl all sts.

Row 3: YO, K1, *K3, K2tog, YO, K3, YO, ssk, K2; rep from * to 2 sts before marker, K2, YO.

Row 5: YO, K2, *K2, K2tog, YO, K5, YO, ssk, K1; rep from * to 3 sts before marker, K3, YO.

Row 7: YO, K1, YO, ssk, *K1, K2tog, YO, K1, YO, ssk; rep from * to 4 sts before marker, K1, K2tog, YO, K1, YO.

Row 9: YO, K3, YO, *SK2P, YO, K3, YO; rep from * to marker.

Row 11: YO, K3, K2tog, YO, *K1, YO, ssk, K7, K2tog, YO; rep from * to 6 sts before marker, K1, YO, ssk, K3, YO.

Row 13: YO, K3, K2tog, YO, K1, *K2, YO, ssk, K5, K2tog, YO, K1; rep from * to 7 sts before marker, K2, YO, ssk, K3, YO.

Row 15: YO, K3, K2tog, YO, K2, *K3, YO, ssk, K3, K2tog, YO, K2; rep from * to 8 sts before marker, K3, YO, ssk, K3, YO.

Row 17: YO, K3, YO, *K2tog, YO, K1, YO, ssk, K1; rep from * to 8 sts before marker, K2tog, YO, K1, YO, ssk, YO, K3, YO.

Row 19: YO, K4, YO, K2tog, YO, K3, YO, *SK2P, YO, K3, YO; rep from * to 6 sts before marker, ssk, YO, K4, YO.

Row 20: Purl all sts.

Rep rows 1–20 for patt.

Chart B

Row 1 (RS): YO, *K4, K2tog, YO, K1, YO, ssk, K3; rep from * to 1 st before marker, K1, YO.

Row 2 and all even numbered rows (WS): Purl all sts.

Row 3: YO, K1, *K3, K2tog, YO, K3, YO, ssk, K2; rep from * to 2 sts before marker, K2, YO.

Row 5: YO, K2, *K2, (K2tog, YO) twice, K1, (YO, ssk) twice, K1; rep from * to 3 sts before marker, K3, YO.

Row 7: YO, K1, YO, ssk, *K1, K2tog, YO, K2tog, (K1, YO) twice, K1, ssk, YO, ssk; rep from * to 4 sts before marker, K1, K2tog, YO, K1, YO.

Row 9: YO, K3, YO, *SK2P, YO, K2tog, K2, YO, K1, YO, K2, ssk, YO; rep from * to 6 sts before marker, SK2P, YO, K3, YO.

Row 11: YO, K3, K2tog, YO, *K1, YO, ssk, K7, K2tog, YO; rep from * to 6 sts before marker, K1, YO, ssk, K3, YO.

Row 13: YO, K3, K2tog, YO, K1, *K2, YO, ssk, K5, K2tog, YO, K1; rep from * to 7 sts before marker, K2, YO, ssk, K3, YO.

Row 15: YO, K3, *(K2tog, YO) twice, K1, (YO, ssk) twice, K3; rep from * to marker, YO.

Row 17: YO, K3, (YO, K2tog) twice, K1, YO, *K1, YO, K1, ssk, YO, ssk, K1, K2tog, YO, K2tog, K1, YO; rep from * to 9 sts before marker, K1, YO, K1, (ssk, YO) twice, K3, YO.

Row 19: YO, K4, (YO, K2tog) twice, K2, YO, *K1, YO, K2, ssk, YO, SK2P, YO, K2tog, K2, YO; rep from * to 11 sts before marker, K1, YO, K2, (ssk, YO) twice, K4, YO.

Row 20: Purl all sts.

Rep rows 1–20 for patt.

Chart C

Row 1 (RS): YO, *K2, (K2tog, YO) twice, K1, (YO, ssk) twice, K1; rep from * to 1 st before marker, K1, YO.

Row 2 and all even-numbered rows (WS): Purl all sts.

Row 3: YO, K1, *K1, (K2tog, YO) twice, K3, (YO, ssk) twice; rep from * to 2 sts before marker, K2, YO.

Row 5: YO, K1, YO, *SK2P, YO, (K2tog, YO) twice, K1, (YO, ssk) twice, YO; rep from * to 4 sts before marker, SK2P, YO, K1, YO.

Row 7: YO, K1, YO, ssk, *K1, (K2tog, YO) twice, K3, (YO, ssk) twice; rep from * to 4 sts before marker, K1, K2tog, YO, K1, YO.

Row 9: YO, K3, YO, *SK2P, YO, (K2tog, YO) twice, K1, (YO, ssk) twice, YO; rep from * to 6 sts before marker, SK2P, YO, K3, YO.

Row 11: YO, K3, K2tog, YO, *K1, (YO, ssk) twice, YO, SK2P, YO, (K2tog, YO) twice; rep from * to 6 sts before marker, K1, YO, ssk, K3, YO.

Row 13: YO, K3, K2tog, YO, K1, *K2, (YO, ssk) twice, K1, (K2tog, YO) twice, K1; rep from * to 7 sts before marker, K2, YO, ssk, K3, YO.

Row 15: YO, K3, (K2tog, YO) twice, *K1, (YO, ssk) twice, YO, SK2P, YO, (K2tog, YO) twice; rep from * to 8 sts before marker, K1, (YO, ssk) twice, K3, YO.

Row 17: YO, K3, YO, (K2tog, YO) twice, K1, *K2, (YO, ssk) twice, K1, (K2tog, YO) twice, K1; rep from * to 9 sts before marker, K2, (YO, ssk) twice, YO, K3, YO.

Row 19: YO, K4, YO, (K2tog, YO) twice, K1, YO, *SK2P, YO, K1, YO, ssk, YO, SK2P, YO, K2tog, YO, K1, YO; rep from * to 12 sts before marker, SK2P, YO, K1, (YO, ssk) twice, YO, K4, YO.

Row 20: Purl all sts.

Rep rows 1–20 for patt.

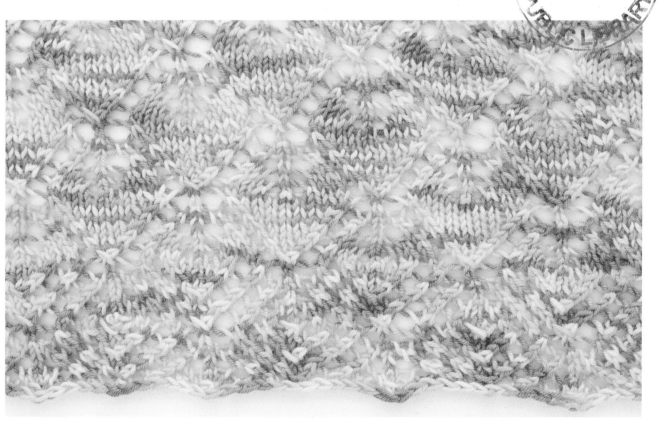

Herbstwald

Set-Up Rows

Work tab CO (page 74) as foll: CO 3 sts. Knit 6 rows. Turn work 90° and pick up 3 sts along edge. Turn work 90° and pick up 3 sts from CO edge. (9 sts)

Row 1 (RS): K3, PM, YO, K1, YO, PM, K1 (center st), PM, YO, K1, YO, PM, K3. (13 sts)

Row 2 (WS): K3, purl to last 3 sts (slipping markers), K3.

Row 3: K3, SM, YO, knit to next marker, YO, SM, K1, SM, YO, knit to last 3 sts, YO, SM, K3.

Work rows 2 and 3 another 4 times. Rep row 2 once more. (33 sts)

Body of Shawl

Cont working first 3 sts and last 3 sts in garter st (knit every row) and working center st in St st (knit on RS, purl on WS). Work chart A between st markers on each half of shawl 3 times total.

Stitch Count	
First rep of chart A	81 sts
Second rep of chart A	129 sts
Third rep of chart A	177 sts

Work chart B between st markers on each half of shawl 3 times total.

Stitch Count	
First rep of chart B	225 sts
Second rep of chart B	273 sts
Third rep of chart B	321 sts

MAKE IT BIGGER!

There are lots of options to make this shawl larger if you have extra yarn. Any of the charts can be repeated to add some length to your shawl.

Lace Edging

Work chart C between st markers on each half of shawl. (369 sts)

Finishing

BO loosely knitwise as described on page 75. With tapestry needle, weave in ends. Using blocking wires or pins, block to finished measurements.

Chart A

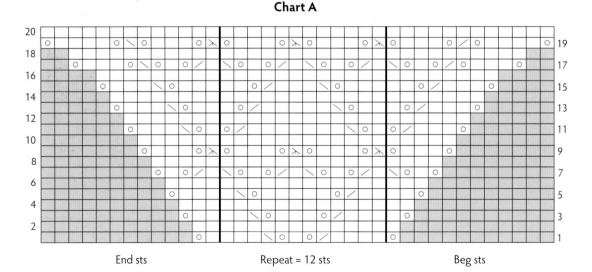

End sts   Repeat = 12 sts   Beg sts

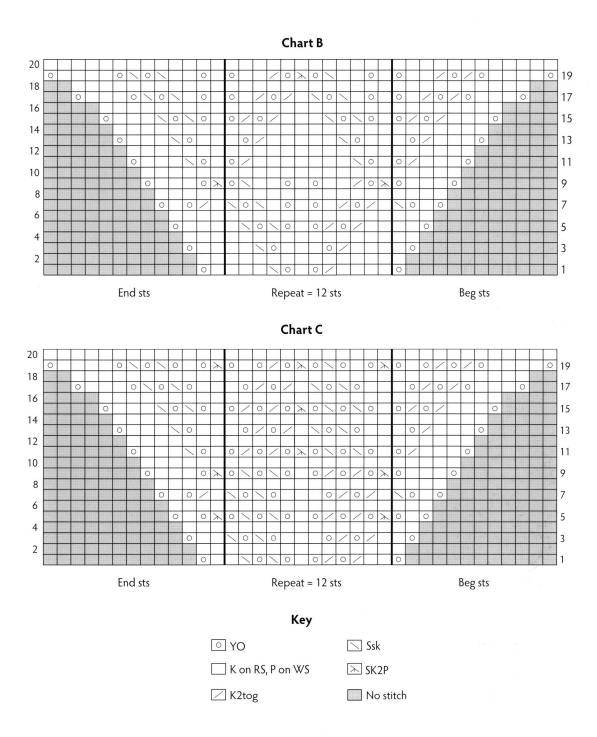

Chart B

Chart C

Key

⊙	YO	⟍	Ssk
☐	K on RS, P on WS	⋏	SK2P
⟋	K2tog	▨	No stitch

Harvey

A simple lace pattern with garter-stitch accents make this shawl a cinch to knit. I grew up in Illinois, on Harvey, a straight-as-an-arrow neighborhood street, for which this shawl is named. You can look for the straight lines in the lace to guide your way and help you keep track of where you are in the pattern.

SKILL LEVEL: Easy ⬤■☐◻

FINISHED MEASUREMENTS: 45" x 18"

Materials

1 skein of Merilon Sock from Black Trillium Fibre Studio (75% superwash merino wool, 25% nylon; 100 g; 437 yds) in color Stan **1**

US size 4 (3.5 mm) circular needle, 24" or longer

4 stitch markers

Tapestry needle

Blocking wires and/or blocking pins

Gauge

18 sts and 40 rows = 4" in garter st

Lace Pattern

See lace chart on page 54, or follow written instructions below.

Row 1 (RS): YO, *K1, YO, SK2P, YO; rep from * to last st, K1, YO.

Row 2 and all even-numbered rows (WS): Purl all sts.

Row 3: YO, K1, *K1, YO, SK2P, YO; rep from * to last 2 sts, K2, YO.

Row 5: YO, K2, *K1, YO, SK2P, YO; rep from * to last 3 sts, K3, YO.

Row 7: YO, K3, *K1, YO, SK2P, YO; rep from * to last 4 sts, K4, YO.

Row 8: Purl all sts.

Rep rows 1–8 for patt.

Set-Up Rows

Work tab CO (page 74) as foll: CO 5 sts. Knit 10 rows. Turn work 90° and pick up 5 sts along edge. Turn work 90° and pick up 5 sts from CO edge. (15 sts)

Row 1 (RS): K5, PM, YO, K1, YO, PM, K3 (center sts), PM, YO, K1, YO, PM, K5. (19 sts)

Row 2 (WS): K5, SM, P3, SM, K3, SM, P3, SM, K5.

Row 3: K5, SM, YO, K3, YO, SM, K3, SM, YO, K3, YO, SM, K5. (23 sts)

Row 4: K5, SM, P5, SM, K3, SM, P5, SM, K5.

Body of Shawl

*Cont working first 5 sts and last 5 sts in garter st (knit every row) and working the center 3 sts in garter st (knit every row). Work lace chart between st markers on each half of shawl 4 times total. Work garter-stitch band as follows:

Row 1 (RS): K5, SM, YO, knit to next marker, YO, SM, K3, SM, YO, knit to last 5 sts, SM, YO, K5.

Row 2 (WS): Knit all sts, slipping markers along the way.

Work rows 1 and 2 another 3 times.*

Work from * to * 2 more times.

Stitch Count			
	First rep of * to *	Second rep of * to *	Third rep of * to *
First rep of lace chart	39 sts	119 sts	199 sts
Second rep of lace chart	55 sts	135 sts	215 sts
Third rep of lace chart	71 sts	151 sts	231 sts
Fourth rep of lace chart	87 sts	167 sts	247 sts
Garter-st band	103 sts	183 sts	263 sts

Harvey

Finishing

BO loosely knitwise as described on page 75. With tapestry needle, weave in ends. Using blocking wires or pins, block to finished measurements.

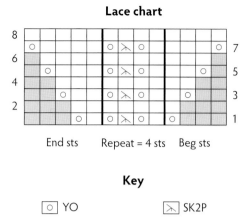

Lace chart

End sts   Repeat = 4 sts   Beg sts

Key

⊙ YO   ⋋ SK2P

☐ K on RS, P on WS   ▨ No stitch

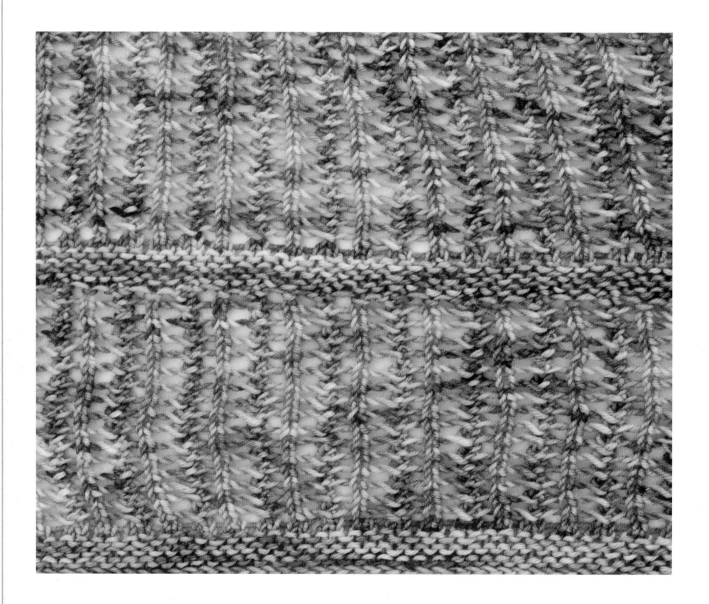

Beyond-the-Triangle Shawls

While the most common type of shawl is worked as a triangle, the options are nearly endless for shawl shapes. In this section the patterns explore styles and techniques that go beyond the top-down triangular shawls found in the previous sections. Here you'll find a bottom-up, short-row shawlette, as well as one worked from side to side. Enjoy the challenge of knitting beyond the triangle!

Vintage Flair

Knit sideways, the lace takes on a whole new look. By adding stitches and then binding them off, you're left with a picot lace edge that will definitely turn some heads.

SKILL LEVEL: Intermediate ⬤■■◻

FINISHED MEASUREMENTS: 52" x 9"

Materials

1 skein of Tosh Sock from Madelinetosh Hand-Dyed Yarns (100% superwash merino wool; 395 yds) in color Golden Hickory ❶

US size 4 (3.5 mm) needles

1 stitch marker

Tapestry needle

Blocking wires and/or blocking pins

Gauge

24 sts and 36 rows = 4" in garter st

Pattern Note

Stitch count will change from row to row. In row 4, you will bind off two stitches, leaving one stitch on the right-hand needle. This stitch counts as the first stitch of the K8 that follows the bind off.

Lace Pattern

See lace chart on page 58, or follow written instructions below.

Row 1 (RS): Sl 1 purlwise wyib, K2, YO, K2tog, YO, K1, (YO, K2tog) twice, YO, K2. (14 sts)

Row 2 (WS): K11, YO, K2tog, K1. (14 sts)

Row 3: Sl 1 purlwise wyib, K2, YO, K2tog, YO, K9. (15 sts)

Row 4: BO 2 sts, K8, K2tog, YO, K2tog, K1. (12 sts)

Rep rows 1–4 for patt.

Set-Up Rows

CO 3 sts. Knit 2 rows.

Row 1 (RS): (K1, YO) twice, K1. (5 sts)

Rows 2 and 4 (WS): Knit all sts.

Row 3: K2, YO, K1, YO, K2. (7 sts)

Row 5: K2, YO, knit to last 2 sts, YO, K2. (9 sts)

Work rows 4 and 5 another 4 times. Rep row 4 once more. (17 sts)

Increase Section

Row 1 (RS): K2, YO, K1, YO, K2, PM, work row 1 of chart to end.

Row 2 (WS): Work next row of chart to marker, SM, knit to end.

Row 3: K2, YO, knit to 2 sts before marker, YO, K2, SM, work next row of chart to end.

Row 4: Work next row of chart to marker, SM, knit to end.

Work rows 3 and 4 another 18 times. (57 sts)

Note: Chart will be repeated a total of 10 times in the increase section.

Body of Shawl

Row 1 (RS): K2, YO, K1, K2tog, knit to 5 sts before marker, K2tog, K1, YO, K2, SM, work row 1 of chart to end.

Row 2 (WS): Work row 2 of chart to marker, SM, knit to end.

Row 3: K2, YO, K1, K2tog, knit to 5 sts before marker, K2tog, K1, YO, K2, SM, work row 3 of chart to end.

Row 4: Work row 4 of chart to marker, SM, knit to end.

Rep rows 1–4 until piece measures approx 32" from CO edge, ending with row 4.

Decrease Section

Row 1 (RS): K2, YO, K1, K2tog twice, knit to 7 sts before marker, K2tog twice, K1, YO, K2, SM, work row 1 of chart to end.

Row 2 (WS): Work row 2 of chart to marker, SM, knit to end.

Row 3: K2, YO, K1, K2tog twice, knit to 7 sts before marker, K2tog twice, K1, YO, K2, SM, work next row of chart to end.

Row 4: Work next row of chart to marker, SM, knit to end.

Work rows 3 and 4 another 14 times. Remove marker on final row. (25 sts)

Row 5: K2, YO, K1, K2tog twice, knit to last 7 sts, K2tog twice, K1, YO, K2.

Row 6: Knit all sts.

Work rows 5 and 6 another 4 times. (15 sts)

Row 7: K2, YO, K1, K2tog twice, K1, K2tog twice, K1, YO, K2. (13 sts)

Rows 8, 10, and 12: Knit all sts.

Row 9: K2, YO, K1, K2tog, K3tog, K2tog, K1, YO, K2. (11 sts)

Row 11: K2, YO, K2tog, K3tog, K2tog, YO, K2. (9 sts)

Row 13: K1, YO, K2tog, K3tog, K2tog, YO, K1. (7 sts)

Row 14: Knit all sts.

Finishing

BO loosely knitwise as described on page 75. With tapestry needle, weave in ends. Using blocking wires or pins, block to finished measurements.

Lace chart

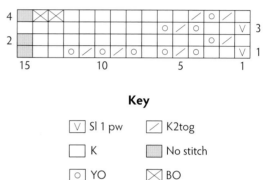

Key

V	Sl 1 pw	/	K2tog
	K		No stitch
o	YO	⊠	BO

Flower Garden

Spring has sprung all over this shawlette. Floral panels running down the edges and center and little flowers at the bottom of the shawl will keep you dreaming of springtime.

SKILL LEVEL: Experienced ● ● ● ◼

FINISHED MEASUREMENTS: 42" x 17"

Materials

2 skeins of Sock-a-Licious from Kolláge Yarns (70% fine superwash merino wool, 10% mulberry silk, 20% nylon; 100 g; 354 yds) in color 7813 Sangria **1**

US size 3 (3.25 mm) circular needle, 24" or longer

6 stitch markers

Tapestry needle

Blocking wires and/or blocking pins

Gauge

22 sts and 32 rows = 4" in St st

Lace Patterns

See charts A and B on page 62, or follow written instructions below. *Note:* Charts only show RS rows.

Chart A

Row 1 (RS): K7, YO, SK2P, YO, K7.

Row 2 and all even-numbered rows (WS): Purl all sts.

Row 3: K6, YO, K2tog, K1, ssk, YO, K6.

Row 5: K5, YO, K2tog, K3, ssk, YO, K5.

Row 7: K4, YO, K2tog, K5, ssk, YO, K4.

Row 9: K4, ssk, YO, K5, YO, K2tog, K4.

Row 11: K5, ssk, YO, K3, YO, K2tog, K5.

Row 13: K2, (ssk, YO) 3 times, K1, (YO, K2tog) 3 times, K2.

Row 15: K3, (ssk, YO) 3 times, K1, (YO, K2tog) twice, K3.

Row 17: K4, (ssk, YO) twice, K1, (YO, K2tog) twice, K4.

Row 19: K5, (ssk, YO) twice, K1, YO, K2tog, K5.

Row 21: K6, ssk, YO, K1, YO, K2tog, K6.

Row 23: K7, ssk, YO, K8.

Row 24: Purl all sts.

Rep rows 1–24 for patt.

Chart B

Row 1 (RS): YO, *K2, YO, K3tog, YO, K3; rep from * to marker, YO.

Row 2 and all even-numbered rows (WS): Purl all sts.

Row 3: YO, K1, *ssk, YO, K3, YO, K2tog, K1; rep from * to 1 st before marker, K1, YO.

Row 5: YO, K2, *K2, YO, K3tog, YO, K3; rep from * to 2 sts before marker, K2, YO.

Row 7: YO, K3, *YO, ssk, YO, SK2P, YO, K2tog, YO, K1; rep from * to 3 sts before marker, K3, YO.

Row 9: YO, K4, *K2, YO, SK2P, YO, K3; rep from * to 4 sts before marker, K4, YO.

Row 11: YO, K5, *K2, YO, SK2P, YO, K3; rep from * to 5 sts before marker, K5, YO.

Row 12: Purl all sts.

Set-Up Rows

CO 63 sts. Knit 3 rows.

Row 1 (RS): K2, *PM, K17, PM, K4; rep from * once, PM, K17, PM, K2.

Row 2 (WS): K2, purl to last 2 sts (slipping markers), K2.

Body of Shawl

Row 1 (RS): K2, *SM, work row 1 of chart A, SM, YO, knit to next marker, YO; rep from * once, SM, work row 1 of chart A, SM, K2. (67 sts)

Rows 2 and 4 (WS): K2, purl to last 2 sts (slipping markers), K2.

Row 3: K2, *SM, work next row of chart A, SM, YO, knit to next marker, YO; rep from * once, SM, work next row of chart A, SM, K2.

Cont working rows 3 and 4 above, working next row of chart A on odd-numbered rows until chart has been worked a total of 4 times (255 sts). Cont working rows 3 and 4 above, working next row of chart A on odd-numbered rows until chart has been worked through row 11 (279 sts). Work row 4 above once more.

Lace Edging

Row 1 (RS): K2, *SM, work next row of chart A, SM, work row 1 of chart B; rep from * once, SM, work next row of chart A, SM, K2.

Rows 2 and 4 (WS): K2, purl to last 2 sts, K2.

Row 3: K2, *SM, work next row of chart A, SM, work next row of chart B; rep from * once, SM, work next row of chart A, SM, K2.

Work rows 3 and 4 another 3 times. (299 sts)

Work row 3 once more. (303 sts)

Knit 1 row.

Finishing

BO loosely purlwise, as described on page 75. With tapestry needle, weave in ends. Using blocking wires or pins, block to finished measurements.

Chart A

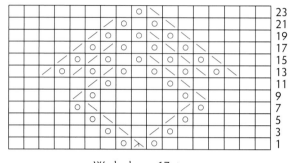

Worked over 17 sts

Chart B

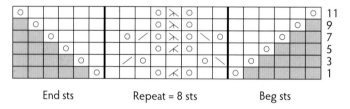

End sts   Repeat = 8 sts   Beg sts

Only RS rows are charted. Purl all sts on WS rows.

Key

○	YO	╱	K2tog
□	K on RS	⋏	SK2P
⋏	K3tog	▨	No stitch
╲	Ssk		

Briargate

Sometimes you have two skeins of sock yarn that seem to go perfectly together. Or maybe you had to barely break into a second skein of sock yarn to finish the toe for that large-footed person in your life. Why not combine them to make a beautiful two-colored shawl?

SKILL LEVEL: Experienced ⬤■■◗

FINISHED MEASUREMENTS: 80" x 12½"

Materials

Caper Sock from String Theory Hand Dyed Yarn (80% superwash merino wool, 10% cashmere, 10% nylon; 113 g; 400 yds) (🔢1)

A 1 skein in color Pewter

B 1 skein in color Mallow

US size 4 (3.5 mm) circular needle, 24" or longer

Tapestry needle

Blocking wires and/or blocking pins

Gauge

20 sts and 36 rows = 4" in St st

Lace Pattern

See lace chart opposite, or follow written instructions below.

Row 1 (RS): K2, YO, K1, YO, *SK2P, YO, K2tog, YO, K7, YO, ssk, YO; rep from * to last 6 sts, SK2P, YO, K1, YO, K2.

Row 2 and all even-numbered rows (WS): K3, YO, purl to last 3 sts, YO, K3.

Row 3: K2, YO, K4, *YO, K3tog, YO, K1, YO, K2, SK2P, K2, YO, K1, YO, ssk; rep from * to last 7 sts, YO, K2tog, K3, YO, K2.

Row 5: K2, YO, K5, YO, *SK2P, YO, K1, YO, ssk, YO, K1, SK2P, K1, YO, K2tog, YO, K1, YO; rep from * to last 10 sts, K2tog, K6, YO, K2.

Row 7: K2, YO, K8, *K4, YO, ssk, YO, SK2P, YO, K2tog, YO, K3; rep from * to last 11 sts, K9, YO, K2.

Row 9: K2, YO, K9, YO, *SK2P, K2, YO, K1, YO, ssk, YO, K3tog, YO, K1, YO, K2; rep from * to last 14 sts, SK2P, YO, K9, YO, K2.

Row 11: K2, YO, K5, (YO, K2tog, YO, K1) twice, YO, *SK2P, K1, YO, K2tog, YO, K1, YO, SK2P, YO, K1, YO, ssk, YO, K1; rep from * to last 16 sts, SK2P, YO, (K1, YO, K2tog, YO) twice, K5, YO, K2.

Row 12: K3, YO, purl to last 3 sts, YO, K3.

Rep rows 1–12 for patt.

Body of Shawl

Set-up rows: With A, CO 125 sts. Knit 2 rows.

Row 1 (RS): Cont with A, K2, YO, knit to last 2 sts, YO, K2. (127 sts)

Row 2 (WS): K3, YO, purl to last 3 sts, YO, K3. (129 sts)

Work rows 1 and 2 another 31 times. (253 sts)

Row 3: K2, YO, knit to last 2 sts, YO, K2. (255 sts)

Row 4: K3, YO, knit to last 3 sts, YO, K3. (257 sts)

Work rows 3 and 4 once more. (261 sts)

Lace Edging

With B, work rows 1–12 of lace chart 3 times total.

Stitch Count	
First rep of lace chart	289 sts
Second rep of lace chart	317 sts
Third rep of lace chart	345 sts

With A, work final edging as follows:

Row 1 (RS): K2, YO, knit to last 2 sts, YO, K2. (347 sts)

Row 2 (WS): K3, YO, knit to last 3 sts, YO, K3. (349 sts)

Rep rows 1 and 2 once more. (353 sts)

Row 3: K1, *YO twice, SK2P; rep from * to last st, YO twice, K1.

Row 4: K1, *(K1, P1) into each YO of double YO, K1; rep from * to last 3 sts, (K1, P1) twice into double YO, K1.

Finishing

BO loosely knitwise as described on page 75. With tapestry needle, weave in ends. Using blocking wires or pins, block to finished measurements.

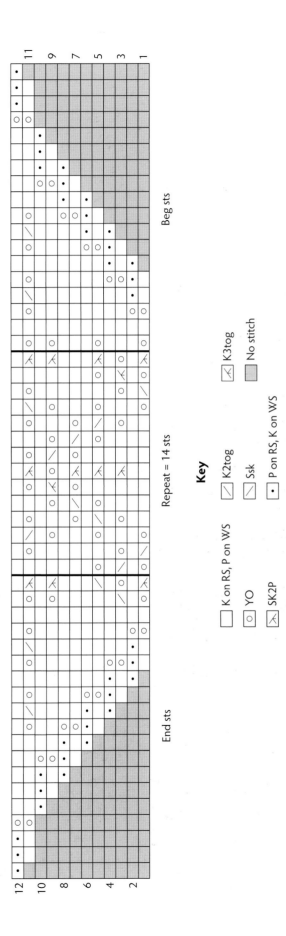

Lace chart

Key

K on RS, P on WS	K3tog
YO	No stitch
SK2P	K2tog
	Ssk
	P on RS, K on WS

Wedgewood

Since we're making shawls knit with sock yarn, why not knit one that uses a common sock-knitting technique? The Wedgewood shawl is knit starting at the lace edge and features short rows to curve the shawl into a crescent shape.

SKILL LEVEL: Experienced ◼◼◼▶

FINISHED MEASUREMENTS: 78" x 10"

Materials

1 skein of Shepherd Sock from Lorna's Laces (80% superwash merino wool, 20% nylon; 100 g; 435 yds) in color 310 Catalpa [1]

US size 6 (4 mm) circular needle, 24" or longer

Tapestry needle

Blocking wires and/or blocking pins

Gauge

16 sts and 40 rows = 4" in St st

Lace Pattern

See lace chart on page 68, or follow written instructions below.

Rows 1, 3, and 5 (RS): K2, K2tog, *K3, YO, ssk, YO, K1, YO, K2tog, YO, K3, CDD; rep from * to 15 sts from end, K3, YO, ssk, YO, K1, YO, K2tog, YO, K3, ssk, K2.

Row 2 and all even-numbered rows (WS): K2, purl to last 2 sts, K2.

Row 7: K2, K2tog, *K2, YO, K2tog, YO, K3, YO, ssk, YO, K2, CDD; rep from * to 15 sts from end, K2, YO, K2tog, YO, K3, YO, ssk, YO, K2, ssk, K2.

Row 9: K2, K2tog, *K1, YO, K2tog, YO, K5, YO, ssk, YO, K1, CDD; rep from * to 15 sts from end, K1, YO, K2tog, YO, K5, YO, ssk, YO, K1, ssk, K2.

Row 11: K2, K2tog, *YO, K2tog, YO, K7, YO, ssk, YO, CDD; rep from * to 15 sts from end, YO, K2tog, YO, K7, (YO, ssk) twice, K2.

Rows 13, 15, and 17: K3, *YO, K2tog, YO, K3, CDD, K3, YO, ssk, YO, K1; rep from * to 16 sts from end, YO, K2tog, YO, K3, CDD, K3, YO, ssk, YO, K3.

Row 19: K3, *K1, YO, ssk, YO, K2, CDD, K2, YO, K2tog, YO, K2; rep from * to 16 sts from end, K1, YO, ssk, YO, K2, CDD, K2, YO, K2tog, YO, K4.

Row 21: K2, K2tog, *K1, YO, ssk, YO, K1, CDD, K1, YO, K2tog, YO, K1, CDD; rep from * to 15 sts from end, K1, YO, ssk, YO, K1, CDD, K1, YO, K2tog, YO, K1, ssk, K2.

Row 23: K2, K2tog, *K1, YO, ssk, YO, CDD, YO, K2tog, YO, K1, CDD; rep from * to 13 sts from end, K1, YO, ssk, YO, CDD, YO, K2tog, YO, K1, ssk, K2.

Row 24: K2, purl to last 2 sts, K2.

Set-Up Rows

CO 383 sts. Knit 1 row.

Lace Edging

Work rows 1–24 of lace chart. (275 sts)

Short-Row Body

Row 1 (RS): K144, turn work.

Row 2 (WS): P13, turn work.

Row 3: K12, ssk, K3, turn work. (274 sts)

Row 4: P15, P2tog, P3, turn work. (273 sts)

Row 5: Knit to 1 st before gap (1 st before previous turning point), ssk, K3, turn work.

Row 6: Purl to 1 st before gap, P2tog, P3, turn work.

Work rows 5 and 6 another 30 times (211 sts); 3 sts remain unworked at each edge.

Next row (RS): Knit to last 4 sts, ssk, K2. (210 sts)

Finishing

BO loosely knitwise as described on page 75. With tapestry needle, weave in ends. Using blocking wires or pins, block to finished measurements.

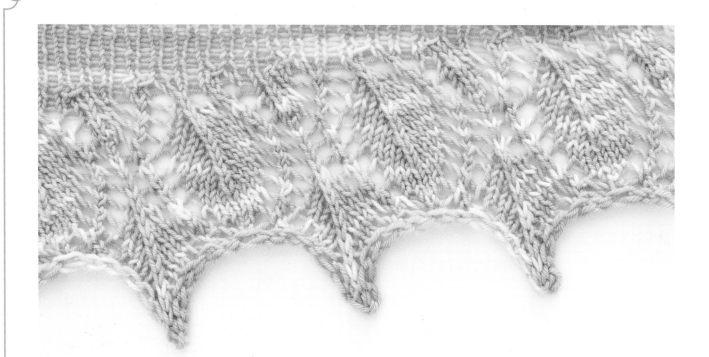

Lace Chart

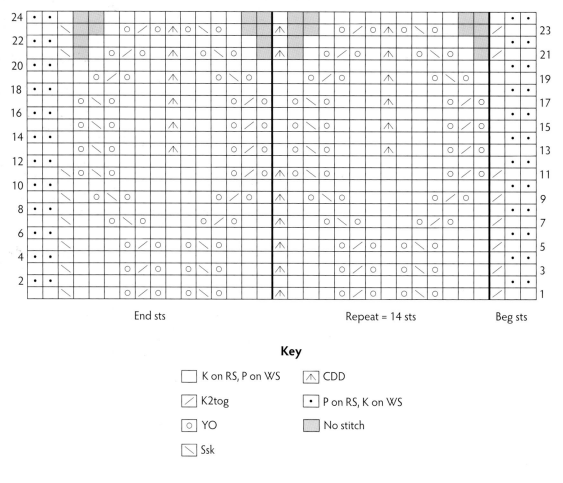

End sts   Repeat = 14 sts   Beg sts

Key

☐	K on RS, P on WS	⋀	CDD
╱	K2tog	•	P on RS, K on WS
○	YO	▨	No stitch
╲	Ssk		

Labyrinth

The combination of a luxurious yarn with the maze-like lace panels running throughout this crescent-shaped shawl will leave you wanting to knit another and another and . . .

SKILL LEVEL: Experienced ■■■◻

FINISHED MEASUREMENTS: 54" x 13"

Materials

1 skein of Entice from Hazel Knits (70% superwash merino wool, 20% cashmere, 10% nylon; 100 g; 400 yds) in color 237 In the Clover 🌀**1**

US size 4 (3.5 mm) circular needle, 24" or longer

6 stitch markers

Tapestry needle

Blocking wires and/or blocking pins

Gauge

20 sts and 28 rows = 4" in St st

Lace Patterns

See charts A, B, and C on page 73, or follow written instructions below.

Chart A

Row 1 (RS): K6, YO, ssk, K2, YO, ssk, K5.

Row 2 and all even-numbered rows (WS): P17.

Row 3: K4, K2tog, YO, K1, YO, ssk, K2, YO, ssk, K4.

Row 5: K3, K2tog, YO, K3, YO, ssk, K2, YO, ssk, K3.

Row 7: (K2, K2tog, YO) twice, K1, (YO, ssk, K2) twice.

Row 9: K1, K2tog, YO, K2, K2tog, YO, K3, YO, ssk, K2, YO, ssk, K1.

Row 11: K3, YO, ssk, K2, YO, ssk, K1, K2tog, YO, K2, K2tog, YO, K1.

Row 13: K4, YO, ssk, K2, YO, SK2P, YO, K2, K2tog, YO, K2.

Row 15: K5, YO, ssk, K2, YO, ssk, K1, K2tog, YO, K3.

Row 16: P17.

Rep rows 1–16 for patt.

Chart B

Row 1 (RS): K1, (K2tog, YO) twice, K1, YO, ssk, K2, (YO, ssk) 3 times, K1.

Row 2 and all even-numbered rows (WS): P17.

Row 3: (K2tog, YO) 3 times, K1, YO, ssk, K2, (YO, ssk) 3 times.

Row 5: K1, (K2tog, YO) twice, K3, YO, ssk, K2, (YO, ssk) twice, K1.

Row 7: (K2tog, YO) twice, K2, K2tog, YO, K1, YO, ssk, K2, (YO, ssk) twice.

Row 9: K1, K2tog, YO, K2, K2tog, YO, K3, YO, ssk, K2, YO, ssk, K1.

Row 11: K1, (YO, ssk) twice, K2, YO, ssk, K1, K2tog, YO, K2, K2tog, YO, K1.

Row 13: K2, (YO, ssk) twice, K2, YO, SK2P, YO, K2, K2tog, YO, K2.

Row 15: K3, (YO, ssk) twice, K2, YO, ssk, K1, (K2tog, YO) twice, K1.

Chart C

Row 1 (RS): YO, *K1, (K2tog, YO) twice, K1, YO, ssk, K2, (YO, ssk) 3 times, K1; rep from * to marker, YO.

Row 2 and all even-numbered rows (WS): Purl all sts.

Row 3: YO, K1, *(K2tog, YO) 3 times, K1, YO, ssk, K2, (YO, ssk) 3 times; rep from * to 1 st before marker, K1, YO.

Row 5: YO, K2tog, YO, *K1, (K2tog, YO) twice, K3, YO, ssk, K2, (YO, ssk) twice, K1; rep from * to 2 sts before marker, YO, ssk, YO.

Row 7: YO, K2tog, YO, K1, *(K2tog, YO) twice, K2, K2tog, YO, K1, YO, ssk, K2, (YO, ssk) twice; rep from * to 3 sts before marker, K1, YO, ssk, YO.

Row 9: YO, K1, K2tog, YO, K1, *K1, K2tog, YO, K2, K2tog, YO, K3, YO, ssk, K2, YO, ssk, K1; rep from * to 4 sts before marker, K1, YO, ssk, K1, YO.

Row 11: YO, K1, (K2tog, YO) twice, *K1, (YO, ssk) twice, K2, YO, ssk, K1, K2tog, YO, K2, K2tog, YO, K1; rep from * to 5 sts before marker, (YO, ssk) twice, K1, YO.

Row 13: YO, K1, (K2tog, YO) twice, K1, *K2, (YO, ssk) twice, K2, YO, SK2P, YO, K2, (K2tog, YO) twice; rep from * to 6 sts before marker, K1, (YO, ssk) twice, K1, YO.

Row 15: YO, K1, (K2tog, YO) 3 times, *K3, (YO, ssk) twice, K2, YO, ssk, K1, (K2tog, YO) twice, K1; rep from * to 7 sts before marker, K2, (YO, ssk) twice, K1, YO.

Set-Up Rows

CO 65 sts. Knit 3 rows.

Row 1 (RS): K3, YO, (K2, YO, PM, K17, PM, YO) 3 times, K2, YO, K3. (73 sts)

Row 2 (WS): K3, purl to last 3 sts, K3.

Body of Shawl

Row 1 (RS): K3, YO, (knit to marker, YO, SM, work row 1 of chart A, SM, YO) 3 times, knit to last 3 sts, YO, K3. (81 sts)

Rows 2 and 4 (WS): K3, purl to last 3 sts, K3.

Row 3: K3, YO, (knit to marker, YO, SM, work row 3 of chart A, SM, YO) 3 times, knit to last 3 sts, YO, K3. (89 sts)

Row 5: K3, YO, (knit to marker, YO, SM, work next RS row of chart A, SM, YO) 3 times, knit to last 3 sts, YO, K3.

Row 6: K3, purl to last 3 sts, K3.

Cont working rows 5 and 6, working next RS row of chart on odd-numbered rows until chart A has been worked 4 times total. (329 sts)

Lace Edging

Row 1 (RS): K3, (work row 1 of chart C to marker, SM, work row 1 of chart B to marker, SM) 3 times, work row 1 of chart C to last 3 sts, K3.

Row 2 and all even-numbered rows (WS): K3, purl to last 3 sts, K3.

Row 3: K3, (work row 3 of chart C to marker, SM, work row 3 of chart B to marker, SM) 3 times, work row 3 of chart C to last 3 sts, K3.

Row 5: K3, (work row 5 of chart C to marker, SM, work row 5 of chart B to marker, SM) 3 times, work row 5 of chart C to last 3 sts, K3.

Row 7: K3, (work row 7 of chart C to marker, SM, work row 7 of chart B to marker, SM) 3 times, work row 7 of chart C to last 3 sts, K3.

Row 9: K3, (work row 9 of chart C to marker, SM, work row 9 of chart B to marker, SM) 3 times, work row 9 of chart C to last 3 sts, K3.

Row 11: K3, (work row 11 of chart C to marker, SM, work row 11 of chart B to marker, SM) 3 times, work row 11 of chart C to last 3 sts, K3.

Row 13: K3, (work row 13 of chart C to marker, SM, work row 13 of chart B to marker, SM) 3 times, work row 13 of chart C to last 3 sts, K3.

Row 15: K3, (work row 15 of chart C to marker, SM, work row 15 of chart B to marker, SM) 3 times, work row 15 of chart C to last 3 sts, K3. (393 sts)

Finishing

BO loosely purlwise as described on page 75. With tapestry needle, weave in ends. Using blocking wires or pins, block to finished measurements.

Chart A

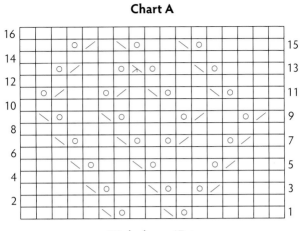

Worked over 17 sts

Chart B

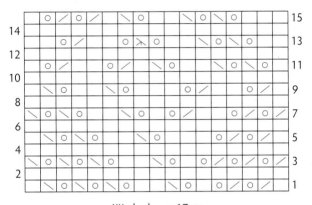

Worked over 17 sts

Chart C

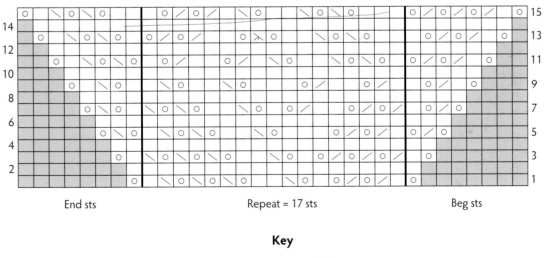

End sts   Repeat = 17 sts   Beg sts

Key

☐ K on RS, P on WS	╱	K2tog
⊙ YO	⋊	SK2P
╲ Ssk	▨	No stitch

Special Techniques

The following techniques are used throughout the book and will help you successfully knit your shawls.

Tab Cast On

The triangle-shaped shawls in the first two sections of this book all begin with a tab cast on. This cast on is typically written as follows:

Cast on three stitches and knit six rows.

Rotate work clockwise 90° and pick up three stitches evenly along the edge. *Try to insert the needle into each of the three bumps on the edge of the tab.*

Rotate work clockwise 90° and pick up three stitches evenly from the cast-on edge (nine stitches total). Turn your work and continue with row 1 of the pattern.

Once the tab cast on is completed, the pattern instructions will read something like this:

Row 1 (RS): K3, PM, YO, K1, YO, PM, K1 (center st), PM, YO, K1, YO, PM, K3. (13 sts)

Row 2 (WS): K3, purl to last 3 sts, K3.

Row 3: K3, SM, YO, knit to next marker, YO, SM, K1, SM, YO, knit to last marker, YO, SM, K3.

Rep rows 2 and 3.

After repeating rows 2 and 3 a few times, you can see the triangle shape starting to form.

Bind Offs

You can bind off your shawl in a number of different ways. The goal is to have a stretchy bind off so that when you block your shawl you can pull and form the edge any way you like. The following are knitwise and purlwise bind offs I always use when finishing my shawls. If you tend to bind off tightly, try using a needle one or two sizes larger. You'll be glad you did—you'll be able to pull the edge of the shawl out when blocking to show off the beautiful points that accent the lace.

Knitwise Bind Off

When binding off on the right side of the work, use the knitwise bind off, also called K2tog bind off. To work, knit the first two stitches together through the back loop. *Slip the stitch from the right needle to the left needle with the yarn in back, and K2tog through the back loops; repeat from * until all stitches are bound off.

Purlwise Bind Off

When binding off on the wrong side of the work, use the purlwise bind off, also called P2tog bind off. To work, *P2tog, slip the stitch from the right needle to the left needle with the yarn in front; repeat from * until all stitches are bound off ending with P2tog.

Blocking

To block your shawl, soak it in warm water, adding a wool wash if you like. After letting your shawl soak, remove and ring it out with a towel. You can use either blocking wires or pins to block it. For a triangular shawl, I like to run a wire along the top edge, and then carefully stretch it out and pin the wires in place on a blocking board to dry. (If you don't have a blocking board, you can pin the stretched-out lace to a carpeted floor.) For the side edges, I run a wire through the points that I want to pull out, and then carefully stretch out the lace and pin the wires in place. For non-triangular shawls, you can either use a variety of wires at different angles, or you can pin each point out individually.

Knitting Abbreviations and Glossary

( )   Work instructions within parentheses in the place directed.

*   Repeat instructions following the single asterisk as directed.

**   Repeat instructions following the double asterisk as directed.

approx   approximately

BO   bind off

CDD   slip 2 stitches together as if to knit 2 together, knit 1 stitch, pass the 2 slipped stitches over the knit stitch—2 stitches decreased

CO   cast on

cont   continue(ing)(s)

foll   follow(s)

g   gram(s)

K   knit

K2tog   knit 2 stitches together—1 stitch decreased

K3tog   knit 3 stitches together—2 stitches decreased

m   meter(s)

mm   millimeter(s)

oz   ounce(s)

P   purl

P2tog   purl 2 stitches together—1 stitch decreased

patt(s)   pattern(s)

PM   place marker

pw   purlwise

rep(s)   repeat(s)

RS   right side(s)

SK2P   slip 1 stitch, knit 2 stitches together, pass slipped stitch over the knit 2 together—2 stitches decreased

sl   slip

sl st(s)   slip stitch(es)—slip stitches purlwise unless instructed otherwise

SM   slip marker

ssk   slip 2 stitches knitwise, 1 at a time, to right needle, then insert left needle from left to right into front loops and knit 2 stitches together—1 stitch decreased

st(s)   stitch(es)

St st(s)   stockinette stitch(es)

tog   together

WS   wrong side(s)

wyib   with yarn in back

yd(s)   yard(s)

YO(s)   yarn over(s)

Useful Information

Metric Conversions

Yards x .91 = meters

Meters x 1.09 = yards

Grams x .035 = ounces

Ounces x 28.35 = grams

Standard Yarn-Weight System

Yarn-Weight Symbol and Category Names	Super Fine **1**	Fine **2**	Light **3**	Medium **4**	Bulky **5**	Super Bulky **6**
Types of Yarns in Category	Sock, Fingering, Baby	Sport, Baby	DK, Light Worsted	Worsted, Afghan, Aran	Chunky, Craft, Rug	Bulky, Roving
Knit-Gauge Ranges in Stockinette Stitch to 4"	27 to 32 sts	23 to 26 sts	21 to 24 sts	16 to 20 sts	12 to 15 sts	6 to 11 sts
Recommended Needle in US Size Range	1 to 3	3 to 5	5 to 7	7 to 9	9 to 11	11 and larger
Recommended Needle in Metric Size Range	2.25 to 3.25 mm	3.25 to 3.75 mm	3.75 to 4.5 mm	4.5 to 5.5 mm	5.5 to 8 mm	8 mm and larger

Skill Levels

■□□□ **Beginner:** Projects for first-time knitters using basic knit and purl stitches; minimal shaping.

■■□□ **Easy:** Projects using basic stitches, repetitive stitch patterns, and simple color changes; simple shaping and finishing.

■■■□ **Intermediate:** Projects using a variety of stitches, such as basic cables and lace, simple intarsia, and techniques for double-pointed needles and knitting in the round; midlevel shaping.

■■■■ **Experienced:** Projects using advanced techniques and stitches, such as short rows, Fair Isle, more intricate intarsia, cables, lace patterns, and numerous color changes.

Resources

Refer to the websites of the following companies to find retail shops that carry yarns featured in this book.

Black Trillium Fibre Studio
www.blacktrillium.etsy.com
Merilon Sock

Cascade Yarns
www.cascadeyarns.com
Heritage

Classic Elite Yarns
www.classiceliteyarns.com
Alpaca Sox

Clover
www.clover-usa.com
Interlocking stitch markers
Split-ring stitch markers

Fiber Optic Yarns
www.kimberbaldwindesigns.com
Foot Notes

Hazel Knits
www.hazelknits.com
Artisan Sock
Entice

Knit Picks
www.knitpicks.com
Gloss

Kolláge Yarns
www.kollageyarns.com
Sock-a-Licious

Lizard Toes Art
http://www.lizardtoesart.com/shop/
Snag-free stitch markers

Lorna's Laces
www.lornaslaces.net
Shepherd Sock
Solemate

Madelinetosh Hand-Dyed Yarns
www.madelinetosh.com
Tosh Sock

Spud & Chloë
www.spudandchloe.com
Fine Sock

String Theory Hand Dyed Yarn
www.stringtheoryyarn.com
Caper Sock

Acknowledgments

There is no way that this book could have been completed without the help of so many people. This was most definitely a team effort.

First I would like to thank my sample knitters, who are not only some of the best knitters I know, but also are some of the most incredible friends I have. Sarah Buehler, Beth Klein, and Melissa Rusk, I am so grateful for your hard work and dedication to this project in addition to all the test knitting you do for me. Jenni Chambers, I am so glad to call you one of my best friends (which is convenient, as you are the fastest knitter I have ever seen). I am so appreciative of all the help you gave me on this project, not only with sample knitting, but also the suggestions and motivation you offered along the way.

I would like to thank Martingale for giving a new designer a chance. I have had a wonderful experience working with all of you and look forward to our future endeavors.

Most importantly, I would like to thank my husband. Alex, you were right beside me and behind me for this whole project. Thank you for being my project manager, my IT help desk, my housekeeper, and my biggest cheerleader through this entire process. And thank you for letting me have power over the remote control while I sat for hours in front of the television knitting shawls for this book.

Thank you all so much. I could not have done this without you.

About the Author

Jen Lucas has been knitting since 2004 and designing since 2008. She has had patterns published with Kolláge Yarns as well as Knit Simple and Classic Elite Yarns. Jen also has a growing number of self-published patterns available on Ravelry. Her designs include socks, shawls, and a variety of accessories.

When not knitting, Jen can be found in the laboratory, testing water. She also enjoys blogging and scrapbooking. Jen lives in the far northwest suburbs of Chicago with her husband, Alex, who has accepted living in a house full of wool.

Find Jen online!

See Jen's designs at: www.ravelry.com/designers/jen-lucas

Read Jen's blog at: www.knittinglikecrazy.com

Follow Jen on Twitter: @knitlikecrazy